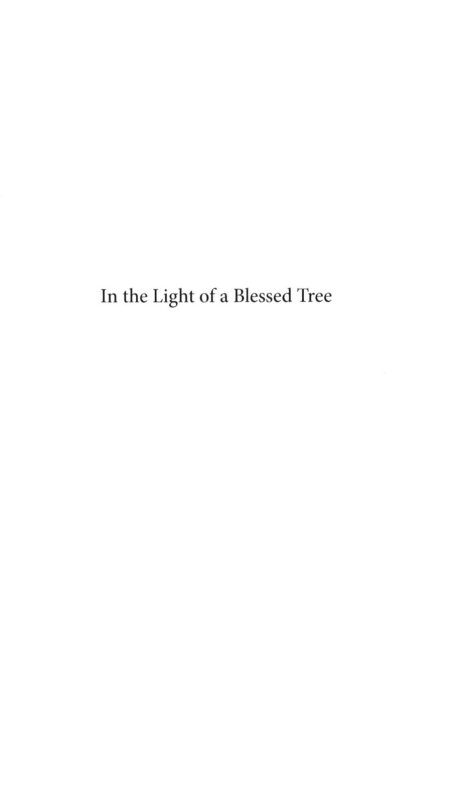

In the Light of a Blessed Tree

In the Light of a Blessed Tree

Illuminations of Islamic Belief, Practice, and History

Timothy J. Gianotti

WIPF & STOCK · Eugene, Oregon

IN THE LIGHT OF A BLESSED TREE
Illuminations of Islamic Belief, Practice, and History

All English renderings of Qur'ānic passages in this book are translated from
the Arabic by the author, unless otherwise noted.

All translations of Hebrew Bible text are taken with permission from the JPS
Hebrew-English Tanakh, the New JPS Translation, 2nd ed. (Philadelphia:
The Jewish Publication Society, 1999[5759]).

Wipf & Stock
An Imprint of Wipf and Stock Publishers
199 W. 8th Ave., Suite 3
Eugene, OR 97401

www.wipfandstock.com

ISBN 13: 978-1-61097-433-2

Manufactured in the U.S.A.

بسم الله الرحمن الرحيم

～

God is the light of the heavens and the earth:
a metaphor for His light is a niche, in which [stands] a lamp;
the lamp is within glass, and the glass [shines] as if it were a
pearly star,
kindled by a blessed tree, an olive
—of neither the east nor the west—
[a tree] whose oil is just at the point of shining forth
though no fire has touched it.
Light upon light!
God guides whomsoever He wills to His light.
God strikes [such] metaphors for the [benefit of] people,
and of all things God is knowing.

～ The Qur'ān, from the *sūra* of Light / *sūra(t) al-nūr* (24):35

In Memory and in Gratitude

THIS BOOK is dedicated, first and foremost, to all of my Catholic teachers who initially opened the gates of learning to me, gates that included the respectful and open-hearted introduction to other faith traditions. My first academic introduction to Islam came from one such teacher while I was just in secondary school, as did my first opportunity to travel in the Muslim world. As I look back with love and gratitude to these teachers, I also see a beaming, great-hearted Jewish teacher standing in their midst, for he was the one who first opened the gates of the Arabic language to me while I was preparing for that first adventure in the Middle East. Although I did not realize it at the time, the Arabic language in turn became the key for opening uncounted other gates, including the gate of my own heart. And so I offer this little book as a modest token of my enduring (if somewhat belated) gratitude to and for these faithful guides.

I also wish to thank my students from the University of Oregon (September 2002–June 2005), whose need made the initial crafting of this book imperative, and my subsequent students at the University of Virginia, York University, and the Noor Cultural Centre in Toronto, Ontario, Canada. Heartfelt gratitude also goes out to Mark Saunders and to Peter and Vanessa Ochs, all esteemed and dear University of Virginia colleagues who breathed fresh enthusiasm into this project when it needed a boost. I offer a special word of thanks to my parents, Jerry and Dolores Gianotti, and my wife, Peggy, for their unwavering support and ongoing sacrifice, and also to my eldest son, Hon-Ming Mustafa, who read and commented on portions of the manuscript. Nancy Shoptaw, my copy editor through Wipf & Stock Publishers, has also earned an honored place here for her caring and careful work on the manuscript. Finally, I wish to express my abiding gratitude to some very dear Canadian friends and supporters, without whom the completion of this slowly-evolving work may not have been possible: the late Dr. Hassanali Lakhani, Samira Kanji, Azeezah Kanji, Romana Mirza, the Hamdani family, and the late Janis Orenstein. Other dear friends and supporters have asked not to be named here, and so I will only say that their contributions to my life and to this book are not anonymous before God.

I release this small offering with the hope and the prayer that it will reflect some of the wisdom and generosity and sacrifice that these luminous souls have shown me.

TJG
Toronto

Contents

Section I: Preliminaries

∽ Prologue ∽
A Word about Illumination / 3

∽ 1 ∽
Getting Started: Facing Ourselves Before
We Turn to Face Islam / 10

Section II: Belief & Practices

∽ 2 ∽
A First Glimpse into the Essence, Belief,
and Mechanics of Islam / 33

∽ 3 ∽
Islam's Sacred Worldview, or Belief System / 42

∽ 4 ∽
Islam's Path of Sacred Action
(Obligatory Religious Practices) / 51

Contents

Section III: History

❧ 5 ❧
The Eastern Branch of the Abrahamic Covenant: Ishmael, the Ka'ba, and the Mythic History of Arabia Prior to the Rise of Islam / 67

❧ 6 ❧
The "Age of Ignorance" and the Dawning of Islam / 79

❧ 7 ❧
Prophecy: Muhammad and the Advent of Qur'ānic Revelations in Mecca / 88

❧ 8 ❧
Archetypes, Prototypes, and the Perfection of Religion: Contemplating Medina as a Prototype for Muslim Societies and a Challenging Articulation of "Real" Islam / 98

Section IV: Experience

❧ 9 ❧
Pursuing Ultimate Horizons: The Mysteries of Being and Becoming "Muslim" / 117

❧ Epilogue ❧
A Few Thoughts on Moses, the Mystic Fish, and Spiritual Education / 131

Bibliography / 133

Section I

Preliminaries

[Remember] when Moses said to his young servant, "I will not give up until I reach the junction of the two seas or have spent a long time [in pursuit]." But, when the pair reached the junction between the two [seas], they forgot about their great fish, which had taken its way in the sea as though through a tunnel. When they had continued on [a while], Moses said to his young servant, "Bring forth our meal, for we have suffered fatigue on account of this journey."

[The servant] said, "Did you see [what happened] when we sought shelter at the rock? I did indeed forget about the great fish. Nothing but Satan caused me to forget to mention it [to you]. It took its course through the sea in an amazing way."

[Moses] said, "That's what we were seeking!" And so they turned back on their tracks, following [the way they had come].

And so they found one of Our servants to whom We had given a Mercy from Ourselves and whom We had taught a [special] knowledge from Our own presence.

∽ The Qur'ān, from the *sūra* of the Cave / *al-kahf* (18):60–65

Prologue

A Word about Illumination

In Medieval times, scriptures and other important texts were often artistically enhanced as a way of displaying the richness and beauty of the text's inner meaning and significance. This process was called "illumination." Departing a little from that venerable tradition, the illuminations found within this little book do not make use of art or calligraphy to magnify, enhance, and reveal; rather, these illuminations come in the form of real-world stories, true accounts that bring key aspects of Islamic belief, practice, and history to life.[1] In so doing, these embellishments reflect and refract the light of many individuals and situations. They draw on my travels across the world, including places such as Saudi Arabia, Pakistan, India, Malaysia, Singapore, Hong Kong, China, Morocco, Jordan, Syria, Israel-Palestine, and many parts of the US and Canada, to name a few; and they emerge from my encounters with a variety of people within a wide range of places and circumstances: from Hong Kong dinner parties to informal gatherings in public libraries and community colleges across rural Oregon; from casual conversations with FBI agents and police officers in

---

1. In order to protect the identity of individuals and institutions mentioned in one or two of the accounts, I have modified peripheral details pertaining to personal or institutional identities. The other details described, however, are true, described in good faith and to the best of my knowledge and/or recollection.

coffee shops and Chinese restaurants to late night spiritual gatherings with Sufi masters in Islamabad, Singapore, Jerusalem, and Toronto; from visiting synagogues and churches across North America to leading Friday prayer services and Islamic history lessons within maximum security US federal prisons; from political and religious exchanges over tea in Palestinian refugee camps to candid conversations around a seminar table in the basement of the Pentagon; from speaking to Canadian Baptist and United Church congregations in Toronto to interacting with Yeshiva students in Israel and learning of their studies there; from negotiating interfaith marriages with local couples and families to helping plan and facilitate international gatherings of religious leaders in India and Israel; from participating in a sweat-lodge as the guest of tribal elders in northern Alberta to having lengthy conversations with Catholic pilgrims on a plane to Tel Aviv; from studying traditional Islamic religious sciences with Jordanian and Palestinian graduate students within the College of *Sharīʿah* at the University of Jordan to participating in Scriptural Reasoning retreats with Jewish, Christian, and Muslim theologians. In every encounter and ensuing discussion, unique insights and understandings have emerged. Each theater of exchange has thus served as a classroom, and each person a teacher. This book, then, textured as it is with some of these experiences, is a small token of gratitude and esteem, humbly offered to my many teachers and to the many settings that have served my ongoing quest for understanding.

This book must also acknowledge a debt to at least one academic crisis: some years ago, as I was just about to begin one of my bread-and-butter "Introduction to Islam" courses at the University of Oregon, I was informed by the bookstore that the main text I had ordered had not yet arrived. A twenty-four-hour panic ensued, during which I tried everything I could think of to make the books appear on the university bookstore's shelves. I failed. The students needed readings, and I had nothing for them. In a university course! Finally, accepting my powerlessness to change the textbook situation, I took upon myself a dreaded task: I began writing a textbook of my own. I wrote daily, intuitively, furiously, and managed somehow to keep my students fully occupied for almost two weeks, at which point the official textbook finally arrived. With much relief on my part, we transitioned smoothly to the newly arrived text, and I gave no further thought to the rapidly written chapters that began our term.

As the class forged ahead, however, students began to complain about the more technical style of the "real" texts I was using and frequently told me how much they had enjoyed the readings of the first two weeks. By the time the class ended, so many such comments had come from so many students that I decided to take a second look at the chapters I had written in such haste. What I found was a more-or-less complete draft of the book you see before you: a short, *very* introductory text that could easily have been entitled, "a crash-course in Islamic literacy," or alternatively "what I think students need to know about Islam in the first two weeks of class."

That is, at any rate, how it was conceived, and—while the text-in-hand is admittedly expanded and much more polished than the first workbook—I have chosen to keep the book close to its original form and spirit. It does not aspire to rival or replace the many fine and thorough introductions to the Islamic religious tradition that abound in our bookstores today. Rather, it seeks to serve the everyday reader, both academic and lay alike, with a first step, after which subsequent steps become easier to choose and easier to manage.

In order to facilitate that unfolding process, this book includes a companion website and blog, where the eager individual will find many additional resources, including topically-arranged guides for further reading in a variety of areas, sample syllabi for more prolonged and systematic studies of Islam, a collection of useful handouts to help navigate one's way through some of the more complex topics, an audio and video library where one can "attend" a variety of lectures, a listing of public events (workshops, talks, discussions, etc.) related to the book and the larger "work" from which this book emerges, and, of course, a place where readers and participants can have a voice.

THE CHALLENGE OF STUDYING RELIGION

Many years ago now, while still a graduate student, I found myself in Edmonton, Alberta, Canada, where two very dear friends were getting married. Encumbered (as usual) with student papers and exams to grade, I worked late into the night at a local café and caught a bus back to my friend's home, where I was staying. As it turned out, I was the only one on the bus, and so the driver caught my attention in the rear-view mirror and began a conversation:

"You look like a religious guy," he said. After I said that, yes, I was actually kind of religious and that I was, in fact, a graduate student in Religious Studies, he asked me to move up a few seats and so began a conversation. He gave me a fairly complete introduction to religion as he saw it: "As far as I am concerned," he concluded, "all roads lead to Rome, you know what I mean?" Thinking that I did get his meaning, I concurred that, in many religions, one can find common ethical teachings and similar insights about reality and human existence. We began to talk about some of those, and as we did the blocks passed swiftly by. When my stop finally arrived, I disembarked and watched him drive his now empty bus off into the night. I remember walking home with a sense of wonder and with the entire conversation reverberating in my mind . . .

How does one talk responsibly about religion? Is it best to focus on common points of ethics and shared insights into the meaning of life? Or is it more responsible to highlight the uniqueness of each tradition with its own history, evolution, rituals, and creeds? Or is religion what people actually do, regardless of what they say they believe?

～

Within the university, the humanities collectively represent a long-standing attempt to study and better understand the human experience in all its complexity. We explore the vast fields of history, art, language, literature, music, philosophy, and other disciplines in order to better understand ourselves: whence we came, how we got here, what we have achieved, where we have gone wrong, what were the reasons underlying our greatest moments of cultural and scientific florescence and our greatest moments of inhumanity, etc. In our quest to understand ourselves, no aspect of human culture is more ever-present than religion, which in many ways represents the universal human need to find meaning, to gain a larger sense of purpose and place in the universe. This yearning to find meaning, a drive that we can identify in almost every culture throughout our history, is perhaps *the* quintessential character trait of the human race, and so to neglect it from our high school and university curricula would be, in some sense, to neglect our very selves.

Seeing the importance of the question, then, there are many ways in which we can go about approaching it. If, by religion, we mean what people actually do or practice, we can approach religion by observing human behavior within a defined culture, time period, and geographical location. For example, based on the lifestyles and practices of a particular group at a particular time in history, we can infer their operative sense of "religion." This is sometimes called an *anthropological* or *ethnographic* or even *popular approach*, a way of engaging religious culture that might take us into the fields of anthropology or sociology or even into the worlds of documentary filmmaking and journalism.

We might, however, be more interested in the historical evolution of a continuous religion or tradition over time, and this interest would give rise to a more *historical approach*, which would witness the gradual growth and transformation of the religious tradition in question as it journeys through time and across cultures. This might be a job description for the historian of religion.

Some seek rather to cut through all or most of these historical and cultural influences in order to get at a core understanding of what a particular religion actually seems to have stood for in its earliest and simplest manifestation. This "core," once uncovered, is then used to judge the extent to which the many centuries of ensuing cultural and historical developments are consistent with the original teachings. Such an approach, sometimes referred to as a *normative approach*, often yields an understanding of a particular religious tradition that is in conflict with many of its popular and cultural manifestations, which are likely to reflect a great many "foreign" influences absorbed through the tradition's journey through centuries and across many geographical, linguistic, and cultural boundaries.

We might also wish to focus on the individual's *experience* of divine mystery within a particular tradition, and this path of enquiry would lead us to a *mystical approach*, which could well include reading spiritual diaries, examining particular practices intended to bring an individual into the mysteries or esoteric aspects of the tradition, studying contemplative poetry and music, or even interviewing spiritually inclined women and men and other inwardly-focused practitioners of a particular tradition. What we find on this path of inquiry might confirm the established dogma of the tradition, or it might challenge the preconceived notions of the majority; in either case, what we find here is a more intimate glimpse of the religious person as seeker—seeker after God, seeker after peace, seeker after knowledge, seeker after an end to loneliness and isolation in a world where separation and individuation dominate our perception.

Of course, our investigation of religion can also involve the study of material culture, art history, music, psychology, neurology, economics, folklore, sociology, political science, area studies, and many other fields of research, and this is what makes Religious Studies so diverse and interesting in terms of the topics and methods it includes. How, then, should we approach the study of Islam?

Any academic attempt to study the Islamic tradition should endeavor to examine "Islam" from a variety of vantage points in an effort to gain a historically and culturally textured understanding of a "tradition" that has thrived and survived in many forms and cultural manifestations and continues to do so in the world today. Short and admittedly incomplete, this little book is intended to serve as the first step of an intellectual journey, be it within an institution of learning, such as a high school, college, or university, or within the larger "school" of one's experience in the world. Wherever and however this text finds you, I hope it proves both accessible and challenging as you embark upon this path of encounter.

∾ *Questions for Reflection and Discussion*

1. How would you define religion?

2. What do you think is most important when studying a religion?

3. What should our criteria be for evaluating it?

4. Do you think that we should NOT look too critically or academically at religion, rather step back and allow it to be? Why or why not?

5. Think of your own religion, if you have one: How do you think people perceived it when it was new and not part of the dominant culture?

6. Coming back to the present: What do you think would be the most "fair" and "balanced" way for someone to study and evaluate your faith tradition today?

7. What should they NOT factor into their assessment? Why?

1

Getting Started

Facing Ourselves Before We Turn to Face Islam

*I*N THE *days and weeks following the atrocities of 9/11, many everyday Americans were so traumatized, fearful, and just plain angry that they began to regard any and every Muslim as somehow being personally responsible for their pain and outrage. As a result, uncounted innocent Muslims in the United States and other western countries found themselves facing threatening behavior and abuse in their workplaces, schools, and communities. On the one hand, they—like all Americans—were shaken by the violence, which left them feeling all the emotions that the nation was feeling: grief, anger, insecurity, etc. On the other hand, as they realized that many of their fellow citizens thought they were involved or somehow responsible for the atrocities, they came to live in fear of their own neighbors, colleagues, and fellow citizens. While there were remarkably (and laudably) few acts of explicit violence against Muslims in the United States, many American Muslims did suffer multiple levels of personal and professional trauma.*

By way of example, following the atrocities of September 11, 2001, a dear friend began to notice that one of her senior colleagues was behaving strangely. Although she had known this colleague to be quite jolly, talkative, and helpful before this, my friend now faced an incredibly sour look whenever she saw him, and he never returned a greeting or even spoke when this friend encountered him in the mailroom or hallway—not even a word. Seeing him relate quite normally with others, my friend began to suspect that this change was restricted to her dealings with this person, and so she became quite puzzled.

My friend had just achieved her first professional milestone, and— suspecting that perhaps this strange treatment was because she had not formally thanked her colleague for his help and sup- port—she decided to pay him a visit and present him a small gift. She did not make it past the threshold. Holding her at the door with his look and his tone, her senior colleague spoke to her forcefully and commanded her never to speak to him unnecessarily again. He said that he was trying his best to be "civil" to her, but he cautioned that my friend should not push it. Beyond what was absolutely necessary for conducting formal business, he wanted nothing to do with her or her professional milestone. "We are not friends," he declared. He then ordered her to get out of his office, which she did—stunned and more puzzled than ever.

My friend was quite distressed and totally in the dark as to why she was being treated in this way. Seeking some understanding and advice, she went to her senior manager and asked whether he knew why their common colleague was so upset. The manager expressed great puzzlement and said that he had no idea. After a few more days had passed in this uncomfortable situation, my friend recalls that, hoping to soften the situation by greeting her colleague in the mailroom, she offered a cheerful good morning. As openly hateful as before, he offered profanities in exchange before storming off.

This went on for several weeks before my friend finally received an email from her colleague, a terse note summoning her to the col- league's office for a "chat." Eager to have some understanding and hopeful for some reconciliation, my friend went. Finally she had the chance to express her bewilderment and asked the senior colleague why he was treating her so rudely. The colleague pointed his finger at her and said flatly, "You are a Muslim." It was an accusation. Remembering that this person had once been a kind supporter and reminding him that their families had dined in one another's homes prior to this, my friend asked, "How can you do this? It's dehumanizing to treat a colleague this way." The colleague replied, "It would only be dehumanizing if you were human to begin with. Now get out of my office." With nothing more to say, my friend got out, never to set foot in that office again.

Although my friend—now very shaken—was just getting ready for a promotion, she never even thought of pressing charges or seeking any professional or personal gain from this rather traumatizing experience with a senior colleague, who, it just so happened, wielded considerable power and influence within the organization at that time. It soon became clear, however, that others—including the senior manager—had been preparing for the worst, even consulting with lawyers in anticipation of some kind of litigation; this became clear in the way they suddenly shifted in their approach to the problem, the way they began referring to the details as "alleged" events and qualified all further discussions in a legalistic manner: "assuming that what you have said actually occurred . . . " became their standard way of responding to her whenever she brought the events up.

Shaken and traumatized now both by the hateful colleague and by the management's disregard, she recalls that, at this point, her workplace felt extremely unsafe. So she began looking for another job far away, somewhere that offered the promise of a safer, less threatening, and slightly less isolating place for her and her young family. She found such a job in such a place, sold her little house, and moved away at the earliest opportunity.

Sadly, this scenario was played out in many places, over and over again following the atrocities of 9/11. Most of these situations were never reported to statistics-gathering institutions, and so the trauma was quietly passed over. The message whispered to American Muslims, even those whose families had been in the United States for generations, was "this is your fault; you are not welcome here."

⌁

Turning to one of my own many experiences, in one of our academic moves, we had arranged to meet with a real estate agent in order to pick up the keys to a house that we had just agreed to rent. When we met the agent, he opened up the house for us and nervously broke the news that our neighbors were, well, Muslims from an Islamic country in Southeast Asia. He quickly went on to assure us that they were actually quite pleasant and well-mannered people who had a child the same age as one of ours and worked for a very reputable employer. Sensing his discomfort in revealing this information about our new neighbors, I cheerfully told him that I had recently given some talks in that country, where I had a wonderful time, and also that, as it turns out, I was—like them—a Muslim, and a professor of Islamic Studies to boot! After a moment of confused contortion, his face and tone changed dramatically. "Oh, that's great!" he said. "You'll get along fine, then!"

I could not help but "bookmark" this in my memory as one more example of how Muslims are often perceived with bias and in a cloud of collective incrimination. It was clear that he initially brought the neighbors up in order to prepare me—a white professional who was assumed to represent the cultural standard—for the shock of my new surroundings.

⌁

Of course, this phenomenon of mass incrimination has spread like wildfire in recent years, especially with all of the controversy and alarmist propaganda surrounding the proposed Islamic center in lower Manhattan, so much so that many people now subscribe to the pernicious and mass-incriminating myth of "the secret Islamic agenda." In other words, many people have come to believe that an overwhelming majority of Muslims in North America and other parts of the Western world are secretly plotting a global conquest in the name of Islam and the subsequent imposition of "Sharī'ah law" upon all (we will take up the topic of sharī'ah in chapter 4). While several examples of this type of alarmist and discriminatory propaganda can be found on the web and on the blog for this book (www.islamicilluminations.blogspot.com), I will briefly summarize just one here for the purpose of illustration.

Like many of the anonymous emails circulating around the web since 9/11, this one seeks to convince everyday Americans that everyday American Muslims support and even celebrate the atrocities perpetrated on September 11, 2001. To anyone with even a little education in Islamic history or theology, this intentionally misleading email seems too ridiculous to merit a response. However, for those millions who have absolutely no knowledge of Islam, it seems very real and very threatening. Such a person sent it (and many such emails before and after) to me in a state of tremendous alarm.

Whatever else can be said about the person who crafted this propaganda, he/she wants us to think that the military conflicts in which America is engaged are part of a larger religious war waged by Muslims everywhere (including within the United States) against the United States. More, he/she is quite willing to grab at anything that looks like evidence and is even willing to misrepresent material (including the sign cited below) to "prove" this assertion.

Beginning with the message, "THIS IS REALITY!!!" the email takes us to a shop in a mall in Houston, Texas, where a sign was posted (and photographed), stating: "We will be closed on Friday, September 11, 2009, to commemorate the martyrdom of Imam Ali (A. S.)." The specific address of the shop is provided immediately under the picture. The email then goes on to say in bold lettering: "Imam Ali flew one of the planes into the twin towers! Nice, huh? Try telling me we're not in a religious war! This has not been around . . . so make sure it does!"

What the average recipient of this alarming message will not know is that Imam Ali has been dead for nearly one thousand four hundred years (he was killed by an extremist in 661 CE). He was the prophet Muhammad's first cousin and son-in-law, and he is revered by Shīʿī Muslims as the first of the blessed Imams, or divinely guided spiritual leaders of the Muslims following the death of the Prophet in 632 CE. The "A. S." following his name means "peace be upon him" and would never be used for any other Ali in Islamic history.

The average reader will also not know that, in the solar year 2009, the anniversary of Imam ʿAlī's death in the Islamic lunar calendar happened to fall on September 11, and so this Shīʿī-owned shop closed in remembrance of that anniversary. As is becoming clear, this somber commemoration had nothing to do with the atrocities of September 11, 2001.

That said, the picture display and brief commentary seem so self-explanatory that they need no academic explanation; in this way, the email takes advantage of people's ignorance and fills them with fear and mistrust of their Muslim neighbors. It is thus the very kind of malicious misrepresentation that leads to the irrational and unfair demonization of an entire group; the very kind of thing that can lead eventually to mass persecution and, if left unchecked, even genocide.

As an educator, I reflect that our greatest enemies in the contemporary world are really ignorance and fear, and such emails are powerful weapons in the service of evil plots to spread both.

Of course, I shared all of this with the person who sent me this email and asked her to be more cautious about spreading this kind of discriminatory propaganda that plays upon people's ignorance and fears. I then urged her to send out a public retraction and apology for this irresponsible and dangerous email, a strong request that was unfortunately ignored. I ended my correspondence by explaining that our shared commitment to stand against racism, religious discrimination, and genocide must include all peoples who are victimized by this kind of hateful misrepresentation. Otherwise, we stand as hypocrites who promote some perpetrators while denouncing others.

~

As with any journey, our odyssey begins here, wherever we may be, and now. For those of us in North America, we begin in a political climate that remembers well the atrocities of September 11, 2001, in a culture that still feels wounded, threatened, fearful, perhaps a little bit vengeful, and still very much at war. Whenever we wish to go somewhere new or seek to understand something new, we must remember that we never really escape ourselves, our place and time, saturated as we are with a multitude of experiences, images, feelings, and assumptions. A classic example of this timeless fact emanates from the writings of James Joyce; even after he left his native Ireland, he wrote of little else. As we will see, this dynamic is particularly important when the "other" in question is Islam, for many powerful images, experiences, emotions, assumptions, and attitudes give color and texture to the way we experience the very word.

If our goal is to try to understand Islam with depth and a sense of academic impartiality, then we have first to become more intimately acquainted with ourselves, each one of us being a partly conscious and partly unconscious conglomeration of many influencing factors. A cynical voice might characterize this conglomeration as cultural or social programming, but let's just leave it as a fact devoid of value judgments for now. The more self-aware we become on this intellectual journey, the more mentally enabled we will be: enabled to remove the lenses of cultural biases and predisposed feelings in order to see things from different vantage points. Note here that I say "different" rather than "better," for the latter is a term loaded with value judgment, and I think it is not the place of a teacher or guide to dictate to you what your experience or concluding judgments should be. As an educator and concerned citizen, my goal in writing this book, then, is to gradually guide you from that which is known and familiar to a point where you can thoughtfully engage something new, something not yet known.

Here, of course, the stranger is Islam, and so, more specifically, I want to bring you to a place where you can have a real encounter with it and draw your own conclusions.

But we race too far ahead. Referring to Islam as an "it" is already a problematic step, for—at least from a scholarly perspective—there are in reality many islams (i.e., many understandings and manifestations of this *spiritual-religious-political* process as it has been and continues to be understood by billions upon billions of people throughout history and in nearly every culture we might encounter). What is Islam? That depends very much upon the one who is being asked. The more pertinent question at the moment, however, is: Who is asking and why?

To answer that question, we must step back and try to examine some of the most fundamental factors that shape the way we come to the question of Islam; we must "unpack" the images, experiences, and cultural assumptions that form the fabric of the way we think about and view the world. In what follows, we will begin to consider a few of these, singled out for their extreme relevance to our quest.

"MODERN"-ITY AND "ORIENT"-ALISM

Using a set of clippers probably as old as he was, the barber and I embarked upon a typical "barber-barbee" conversation. I asked him if the recession was affecting his business; he replied with a grin and a touch of old-country accent, "We don't manufacture automobiles here." I laughed and the conversation took off from there. Eventually, as he sheared the sides of my head with my preferred number one setting, he asked me the inevitable question, "So, what do you do?" As soon as I told him I was a professor of Islamic theology and philosophy (who also worked in Christian and Jewish thought, I added in part to make him feel more at ease), he said, "Those are crazy people over there . . ." Covering his face with his free hand, he went on, "Covering their women like this, killing people who criticize their religion . . . those are crazy people." I tried to explain that the global Muslim population was vast and diverse, but he would hear none of it. "Christianity modernized; they had to modernize. Judaism modernized; they had to, too. But those people, they refuse to modernize. If you tell them, though, they'll kill you, so watch out," he warned me with a smile.

"Look at what happened with those cartoons! They went crazy when that guy drew pictures of Mohammed. And remember that other guy who wrote the book about Mohammed's wives or sisters or whatever? What was his name? Rashi or Rishi or something like that . . ." I jumped in to tell him the name he was looking for, and he continued. "Now we don't like it when people say Jesus was married, or Jesus was gay, or whatever . . . but we don't go out and kill 'em. We don't have to like it, but we let 'em say it. That's because we're modernized. But those people, their crazy. They aren't modern."

Most of us who live within North America or Western Europe perceive of ourselves as "modern" people, just as we regard our nations as "modern" nations, marked by fairly high technological standards, ready access to basic services and information, swift and efficient modes of transportation and communication, a shared sense of future orientation, a shared narrative of global progress, and a shared secular ideal that allows many different religions and ethnicities to live together under a single rule of law, which protects religious identity even as it prevents that identity from dominating the national culture. While the realities of Western life might not always live up to these ideals in all cases, we nevertheless tend to think of ourselves as an advanced or evolved civilization, infinitely farther ahead and better off than more "primitive" societies in the "developing" or "third" world. This way of viewing history in the light of social progression is one of the hallmarks of a complex cultural mindset that scholars call "modernity."[1]

While we may not have had the inclination to step back and examine our shared or popular concept of modernity, we have nevertheless lived within its basic assumptions, and it is important to stop and explore it a little. Modernity comes historically as a fruit of eighteenth-century intellectual/social/cultural trends known collectively as the "Enlightenment." Emerging in a Europe traditionally dominated by the political and intellectual power of the institutional Church, the Enlightenment marked the historical process by which reason rose above all competing authorities and religion was stripped of its power to dominate and determine every aspect of culture, including scientific, philosophical, and artistic expression. As a result of this radical shift in cultural values and norms, religion became relegated to serving as an *aspect* of one's culture rather than the defining force within collective culture; religious beliefs came under the scrutiny of reason and became restricted to the realm of one's private life, even as the public sphere was freed to find meaning independently, without the overt influence of nobles and kings, on the one hand, and priests, bishops, and other religious authorities, on the other.

In the words of Immanuel Kant, one of the greatest minds in the age of the Enlightenment, the Enlightenment marks the historical "coming of age" or maturation of humankind, which had hitherto been imprisoned within a cage of fear and lifelong immaturity:

> It is so easy to be immature. If I have a book to serve as my understanding, a pastor to serve as my conscience, a physician to determine my diet for me, and so on, I need not exert myself at all. I need not think, if only I can pay: others will readily undertake the irksome work for me. The guardians who have so benevolently taken over the supervision of men have carefully seen to it that the far greatest part of them (including the entire fair sex) regard taking the step to maturity as very

---

1. For a more systematic, sociological investigation into the meaning of modernity, one might consult Anthony Giddens, *Consequences of Modernity*.

dangerous, not to mention difficult. Having first made their domestic livestock dumb, and having carefully made sure that these docile creatures will not take a single step without the go-cart to which they are harnessed, these guardians then show them the danger that threatens them, should they attempt to walk alone. Now this danger is not actually so great, for after falling a few times they would in the end certainly learn to walk; but an example of this kind makes men timid and usually frightens them out of all further attempts.[2]

If the Enlightenment marks the throwing off of these controlling factors and the shattering of the old paradigm, modernity marks the establishment of a new order in which unrestrained human reason is given the mastery over everything, including religion. Social scientists and scholars of modernity refer to this restriction or circumscription of religious authority as the "secularization" or privatization of religion, and they see it as one of the hallmark characteristics of modern life. Today we may refer to it more simply as "secularism," but—whatever we wish to call it—there is no doubt that the social scientists are, on the whole, correct in their assessment: secularism, even for those of us who regard ourselves as religious types, shapes the world in which we live even as it shapes the way we think. Secularism is the very foundation for our official separations of church and state and is the main criterion by which we judge a belief system to be "rational" or modern (i.e., suitable for the time in which we live).

In other words, if a religion is seen to accommodate contemporary culture and abide by the rules of secular society, and if it does not interfere with the living of a "normal," rational, secular life and the fulfillment of one's basic civic duties, then we might be inclined to award it high praise as a "moderate" and "reasonable" religion. We might even be inclined to describe it as modern and possibly even "progressive," a term that often signals for us highest honors.

2. This is taken from his essay, "What is Enlightenment?" as published in the December issue of *Berlin Monthly*, 1784.

If, on the other hand, a religious movement or belief system refuses to bow to secularism by rejecting the separation of the sacred from the secular and insisting that religion must determine all or most aspects of our social and cultural life, then we might be inclined to see it as backward, old-fashioned, not at all modern. Such a system might well bring strict rules of ritual purity, gender separation, dietary laws, codes of dress, and other restrictive beliefs and practices into the public sphere, where such manifestations of religious commitment may be regarded as unseemly, irrational, even antithetical to the forward march of modern society. We have only to look at the legal moves against headscarves and face-veils in Europe and North America or the lawsuits opposing the construction of mosques in America or the recent legal ban on Jewish and Islamic practices of ritual slaughter in the Netherlands to see examples of Modernity's judgment of religion in our midst.

Before we go further, it is important to stop and say that this devotion to the ideal of secularism does not describe the worldview of each and every American, Canadian, or European; it does, however, paint the overall landscape of our post-Enlightenment, industrialized world. Indeed, this landscape is so influential within Western culture that western nations have long sought to export it to other countries and cultures. Many see the struggles in Afghanistan and Iraq to be explicit attempts to bring the Western ideal of the socially progressive secular way of life to societies whose systems have not yet "evolved" to our degree. This national or hemispherical desire to bring secular democracy to the world has even been likened by some to a religious-like mission to bring our social "truth" to the world and so recreate its societies in our own image.

It does not serve us here to condemn or praise this devotion to secularism, but it does serve our end to become aware of it and to begin to see how this may color the way we view other cultures and religions. For a religion to be acceptable and esteemed within a secular culture, it has to behave itself by remaining within the boundaries that our society places upon it. The moment religion begins to step out of the private sphere it becomes suspect and runs the risk of gaining a reputation of extremism, backwardness, and maladjustment to the modern world.

Coupled with this is another cultural element that is similarly, invisibly infused into the very air we breathe: coined as "Orientalism" by its most famous critic, the late Columbia University Professor Edward Said (1935–2003),[3] this element essentially represents a centuries-long Western European tradition of depicting the Arab-Islamic world and other Eastern societies (the "Orient") as a single, monolithic "place" where, unlike the West, the inhabitants are treated as essential components of one mindset or ideology or character. Empowered by eighteenth-century European colonialism and political/economic domination of most of North Africa, the Middle East and Far East, this Western phenomenon included the scholarly grouping of many Eastern cultures under the academic banner of "Oriental Studies," the field in which Western scholars became scientific experts of the languages and cultures and texts of these subjugated societies. The living results of this can be seen, for example, in the well-regarded American academic association, the "American Oriental Society," the "Faculty of Oriental Studies" at Oxford, and even the "Oriental Institute" at the University of Chicago, where "Oriental" refers only to Near Eastern languages, history, and archeology. Outside of academic circles, the phenomenon of "Orientalism" also included a popular, western fascination with the Orient, a fascination that often projected exotic fantasies upon the Oriental world, where many westerners imagined harems to be commonplace and

3. Born to a Palestinian Christian family in Jerusalem during the British Mandate, Said's family moved to Cairo in 1947. He eventually made his way to the Unites States, where he won degrees from Princeton and Harvard and became a celebrated professor of English and Comparative Literature at Columbia. His 1978 book *Orientalism* vaulted him to international fame, where he has remained ever since.

everyday "Orientals" to be mystically inclined, although techno-logically and socially backward.

Orientalism, as described by Said and others, is thus a form of racism—indeed, a centuries-old and persistent tradition of rac-ism—that continues to be manifest in the way Western culture thinks about, talks about, and portrays "the East" in general and Arab-Islamic societies in particular. For evidence, we need go no further than mainstream Hollywood depictions of Arabs and Muslims, who are frequently depicted as turban-wearing villains or terrorists, or perhaps as child-stealing, abusive husbands, or as dim-witted, superstitious, premodern characters, as oppressed wives and daughters, or as sultry harem vixens attending submis-sively to *shaykhs* (sheiks or sheikhs), or as hotheaded, semi rational, unshaven men who suffer from serious anger management prob-lems. Jack Shaheen's book, *Reel Bad Arabs: How Hollywood Villifies a People*, is an eye opening study of such Hollywood portrayals of Arabs, which can be seen as popular expressions of Said's thesis.

Beyond academia and beyond Hollywood, we do not need to search very far these days to find explicit depictions of Islam as a hateful and singular "ideology" rather than as a proper religion, such as Christianity or Judaism, with a wide variety of contem-porary interpretations and historical manifestations. Indeed, the public denouncing of Islam as terrorism is often applauded as a courageous, politically-incorrect declaration of obvious truth, whereas Christian or Jewish episodes of violence are seen as anomalies and not in any way representative of the mainstream religions or their communities. This double standard—seeing ourselves as complex, modern, and resistant to stereotypes while seeing Arabs and Muslims as all fitting into a single character-type or premodern mentality—is precisely the charge Said advanced with his publication of *Orientalism*. Needless to say, his academic charge awakened both strong support and strong criticism, but, once made, the charge has never faded away.

~ Questions for Reflection and Discussion

1. What does being "modern" or "enlightened" mean *to you*? Is there such thing as a "modern" religion? If so, what might it mean for a religion to be modern or even progressive? Are the two synonymous?

2. How do you think being a part of your society and historical moment influences the way you approach other cultures, especially ones that are very different from your own?

3. How do you think being "a child of modernity" influences the way you think about other religions? For example, does living within a democratic and secular society, where the people make the laws, make you feel that religion should, in turn, be democratic or more democratically run? How does the idea of an all-powerful, all-knowing deity making the laws strike you?

4. Is it possible for you or anyone to study other societies and religions (even those of the past) without making judgments? How can we come to know other cultures and belief systems in an unbiased or at least fair-minded manner?

5. What do you think of Kant's assertion that humans are doomed to live an immature, intellectually infantilized life so long as they allow themselves to be directed and influenced by religious authorities? Can one be both intellectually "mature" and religious? How?

6. Do you think "Orientalism" is a reality? What are the images and ideas you naturally or instinctively associate with Arabs, Muslims, and Islam? Equipped with pen and paper, sit down quietly for fifteen or twenty minutes. Try to clear your mind of all thoughts and distractions, and then introduce the words "Arab" and "Islam" and "Muslim" to your still mind. Let thoughts and images stream through the pen without stopping to process or evaluate them. Try not to censor yourself,

and remember that there is no "right" or "wrong" attached to whatever comes out. Once you have done this for fifteen minutes, go over the pages you have now filled with words, images, and emotions. What do you find? Is it, on the whole, positive or negative in the way it responds to the words or concepts of Islam and Muslim? Once you have done this, you can ask, where did all this stuff come from?

THE MEDIA

Some years ago, when I was teaching a course in world religions at Penn State University, I had an exchange with a student while we were beginning to study Islam. He began speaking authoritatively about the miserable condition of women in the Middle East, and—interested to hear more—I asked him which countries he had been to. It turned out that he had never visited the Middle East (or even been outside the United States for that matter), and so I asked him, "Well, then, it's a good thing that you have known Middle Eastern women who have described to you their life in the region, right?" He admitted that he had never spoken to a Middle Eastern woman, let alone one who had a scarf on her head. I then asked him, "If you have never visited the Middle East and have never encountered a woman from the Middle East or any 'Islamic' country, how can you speak so authoritatively about the status of women in the region or in the Islamic religion?" He replied simply that it was common knowledge. Everyone knew this for fact. The universal oppression of women in Islam needed no corroboration.

Around that same time, my wife and I traveled with our young son to Hong Kong, where my wife grew up and where her parents still reside. One night, at a dinner party hosted by one of her lifelong friends, we fell into a conversation about Saudi Arabia (this kind of thing always seems to happen to me). Of course, all of the standard stereotypes came out, and everyone there was absolutely certain that all of the stereotypes were absolutely true. Of course, no one there had ever traveled to the Middle East or spoken to a Saudi woman.

Acknowledging that the oppression of women is a problem in the Middle East, just as it is in Chinese culture and in cultures all over the world, I began to explain that the stereotypes frequently do not represent the realities: certainly not for everyone and perhaps not even for the majority. As it happened, we had just been the dinner guests of a real-life Saudi family the day before our departure for Hong Kong, and so I said, "Well, you know, we were just with a Saudi family in their home for dinner a few days ago, and this particular family seemed to have quite a few strong and outspoken women who did not seem oppressed in the slightest degree." Knowing that they were convinced that I was an unabashed apologist, I sent them to ask my wife about it, for she was a childhood friend, and they trusted her. After several minutes of interrogation, they came back to me rubbing their chins and struggling to make sense of my wife's account. "This must be an exception," they concluded. We then found other subjects to talk about.

∾

These encounters, and many others not recorded here, have shown me that no one comes to the subject of Islam "cold" or blank. We all have images, ideas, and feelings about Islam, and all of them color the way we encounter additional images and bits of information. Where do these images and feelings come from? Are they reliable as foundational building blocks for forming opinions about Muslims and their belief system?

I often ask students and other groups to pretend, just for a moment, that they have no knowledge of Christianity other than what they have managed to glean from front-page newspaper articles and major news networks. I then ask them what kinds of stories and images are left to give a picture of the Christian religion? Invariably, stories of pedophile priests and lawsuits against the Catholic Church are mentioned, along with controversies and schisms within America's conservative Christian congregations, the divisive questions of gay ordination and same-sex marriage, militant groups, such as David Koresh's Branch Davidian community and the FBI/Branch Davidian standoff in Texas (rapidly becoming ancient history for today's students), angry clashes between pro- and anti-abortion activists, etc. Once in a while, a sympathetic lead story emerges concerning the Pope's health or his international activism, Mother Teresa's life and death, the making of a movie such as *The Passion of the Christ*, or other similarly benign or noncontroversial topics, but most of the main news attention remains negative, involving scandal, schism, violence, controversy, or unusual developments and strange movements.

These images, if they were *all* we had to go on, would give us a very partial and rather warped understanding of Christianity. They would give us little, if any, insight into the fundamental mysteries celebrated by Christians or what it means for most to lead a Christian life. For example, in all of this media coverage, would one ever get the message that Christian belief is anchored in the doctrine of a Divine love for humanity that is so strong that God became incarnate to suffer, die, and rise from the dead in order to redeem humankind from the otherwise inescapable doom of sin?

This exercise thus brings us face-to-face with a fundamental truth about journalism and the media: they do not have our overall education as their mandate. Rather, they seek to inform us about what is happening in the world with an eye for the unusual, the violent, the controversial, for this is what we collectively regard as "newsworthy" material within our culture. Who has the time to read a front-page article about a Palestinian father Muslim who works three menial jobs so that he can send his children to a Quaker school? Such stories, while real and worthy of being told, do not make the grade in our mainstream journalistic climate, which thrives and prospers on being exciting, shocking, sensational.

Now, in the case of Christianity, most people in the Western world, even those who do not identify as Christians, know enough about Christians and the Christian religion to see the headlines and television images for what they truly are: shocking scenarios and controversial stories that represent neither the Christian faith nor the majority of Christians across the globe.

In the case of Islam, however, we are in a nearly opposite position. Many Americans have never met a Muslim, let alone read a fair-minded book about Islam or taken a class in it during their university or college years. So, when confronted with the terrifying images of angry social demonstrations, suicide/homicide bombings, beheadings, and turban-wearing international villains spewing religious rhetoric of hatred and homicide, we have no way to contextualize what we are seeing. It looks to us that "they" *all* must be like this or, at the very least, must share some complicity in the horror by tolerating it in their mosques and communities. We are left feeling that the hatred and hostility is widespread and growing among the world's Muslim populations, for we rarely hear about "moderate" Muslims standing up in opposition to these frightening media images and personalities.

I am often asked why, since September 11, 2001, no prominent Muslim clerics and organizations have stepped forward to condemn the atrocities perpetrated in the name of Islam. I respond by explaining that, in all my travels and encounters with prominent Muslims in these past years, even in places such as Mecca and Medina, I have yet to find a scholar or religiously learned official who does *not* condemn these atrocities. Incredulous, people ask why they have not seen this in their newspapers or on their televisions, and I have to say that I don't know why. Perhaps it is just that such stories are not as "newsworthy" as the more sensational events involving violence, oppression, and severe rhetoric. In short, who wants to read front-page articles about moderate, peace-loving, and otherwise rather unremarkable Muslims?

All this is, of course, is not to deny that there is a problem or that the violence and the extremism and the terror are real. Sadly, the press does not need to create fantastic fabrications to serve its taste for the sensational and the extreme. Rather, we simply raise here the obvious (although often missing) question: To what extent are these unhappy stories and frightening images representative of the Islamic faith or the one billion or more Muslims scattered all over the world?

⌖ A Personal Media Experience

For the next week or weeks, try to be conscious of the mainstream media's coverage of religion in general and Islam in particular. What are some of the most prominent headlines, stories, and images you see? What trends do you see? Pay particular attention to the way Islam makes its way into the news. What kinds of issues win a place for Islam on the front page or on the headline news broadcasts? What kinds of stories and issues get relegated to the back corners of the paper or never get covered at all?

Section II

Beliefs and Practices

Moses said to him: "May I follow you on the condition you teach me something of that which you have been taught by way of true guidance?"

He said, "But surely you will not be able to hold patience with me [if I take you on]. How can you be patient regarding that which is outside of your knowledge [and] experience?"

Moses said: "God willing, you will find me [to be] patient: nor shall I disobey you in any way."

[The Guide] said: "If then you [choose to] follow me, do not ask me about anything until I speak to you about it."

So the two started off [and journeyed] until, as they boarded the boat, [the guide] punched a hole in it. Moses said, "Did you sink it in order to drown those in it? You have done something senseless!"

He said: "Did I not say that you would not be able to remain patient with me?"

Moses said: "Forgive me for forgetting! Do not be excessive in what you demand of me in such difficult circumstances!"

∼ The Qur'ān, from the *sūra* of the Cave / *al-kahf* (18):66–73.

2

A First Glimpse into the Essence, Belief, and Mechanics of Islam

*T*HE SUMMER *of 1982 was a tense time in the Middle East, especially on the eastern shore of the Mediterranean, where the state of Israel was mounting a major offensive deep into Lebanon, in response to the attempted assassination of its ambassador to the United Kingdom by the Lebanon-based Abu Nidal wing of the Palestinian Liberation Organization (PLO). More or less unaware of what was going on at the time, I was busy going to school in Portland, Oregon, playing sports, and working to save money for my first trip to this "exotic" part of the world.*

I was seventeen, between my junior and senior years in high school, and I had a working knowledge of maybe fifty or sixty Arabic phrases and polite expressions, thanks to Lew, my Jewish teacher and friend who was academically trained in Arabic. Traveling with my world religions teacher/soccer coach/Catholic priest/friend and three classmates (all fellow students and soccer players), I had a very limited understanding of the region, with all its complex histories, indigenous cultures, conflicts, and religions.

The Cairo airport welcomed the five of us to this new world in June of 1982. The extreme heat of the Egyptian summer (often exceeding 125 degrees Fahrenheit) was something of a shock for a young student who had spent most of his life in the relatively cool, damp climate of Western Oregon. Cairo assailed us as a crazy, chaotic, overcrowded, baking, and dusty city, and yet there seemed to be a hidden serenity about the place, especially when the call to prayer—a kind of otherworldly chant it seemed—sounded through the city at prayer times (five times per day). The people we met on the street seemed happy and cheerful, often greeting us, telling jokes, repeating advertising slogans they had memorized in English, and inviting us into their homes and shops for tea. The men mostly wore clean, white cotton robes or white dress shirts with slacks while the women walked past in a wide variety of attires, from traditional dress to Western-style outfits. Without exception, the Egyptians we met seemed delighted by our presence in their country, and so I re-member it as a wonderful and exciting time, filled with lively and pleasant encounters.

Even more impressive to me at the time, most of the people were fasting, for it was the month of Ramaḍān, an entire lunar month (new moon to new moon) during which every able-bodied, adult Muslim is obligated to fast (no food, water, smokes, or other physi-cal pleasures during the daylight hours—predawn light to sunset). The heat of those afternoons in the streets of Cairo or touring the Pyramids outside the city made us feel as if we were inside an oven, I remember, and we lived for air conditioned retreats to hotel lobbies, retreats that most of the people living there could not afford. As they fasted, we consumed liter after liter of bottled water and spent whole afternoons in our hotel rooms when we could take no more of the summer heat.

A "MONASTIC" SOCIETY

Perhaps the most memorable moment of those first days among the Egyptians came one Friday noon when I was out on the city's streets. Friday is the "day of gathering," the day of congregational prayer in the mosque, a religious obligation that even lax and semi-observant Muslims make a special effort to keep during the holy month of

Ramaḍān. The mosques of Cairo overflowed that day, and so I witnessed hundreds of people around me laying newspapers on the sidewalks and the streets in order to perform their prayers right there (Muslims are required to pray on clean surfaces, even clean grass or clean earth, and so the newspapers sufficed as a clean cover for the dirty sidewalks and streets). Right there, totally unaware of me standing by, they prayed, shoulder to shoulder in wide-reaching lines, bowing, standing, sinking to their hands and knees and placing their foreheads on the ground, all together in perfect synchronization.

Now, as a boy, I had always been quite serious in matters of religion. Fortunately for someone of my interests, the Catholic experience of my youth included a strong educational system, within which I was both allowed and encouraged to read a vast range of books, from the Bible to books about Native American heroes, Hinduism, Buddhism, Hermann Hesse novels, good science fiction and fantasy (J. R. R. Tolkien, C. S. Lewis, Ursula LeGuin, and others), and anything I could find dealing with other cultures and religious traditions. It also gave me access to mystical writers and monastic communities, most importantly the Trappist or Cistercian community, which had an abbey within easy reach of Portland. In the course of my high school years, I had been a guest of the monastery on many occasions and had always admired the way their lives revolved around prayer and the remembrance of God; from the moment they awoke in the early morning to the final moments of the waking night, they stopped periodically to remember God, to sing God's praise, to recall their place and purpose in the world.

So, when faced with this rather awe-inspiring sight of a crowd stopping in the midst of the Cairo noon frenzy in order to remember God, to obey the Divine command, and to recall the ultimate purpose of their worldly existence, an insight came: this is just like the monastery, I thought, but a monastery for everyone—for everyday women and men, for young and old alike—a monastic society. This first impression has remained with me ever since, an intuitive vision of a religious and social force so compelling that it managed to establish a whole civilization built around the continuous remem-brance of God. That afternoon on the streets of Cairo, perhaps, was the experience that planted the seed that eventually sprouted into a formal study of Arabic, led to many more visits to the Middle East, and, eventually, inspired me to my do master's and doctoral work in the field of Islamic Studies.

THE FAITH AND PRACTICE OF ISLAM

The word Islam comes from the Arabic verbal noun *"al-islām,"* which means, quite literally, the act of surrendering or submitting oneself to someone or something, here understood to be the act of surrendering oneself to God. This, in the Qur'ān (the "recitation" believed to have been revealed to the prophet Muhammad), is understood to be the primordial religion of humanity and the ba-sic religion of all the prophets, including Adam, Noah, Abraham, Moses, Jesus, and, finally, Muhammad. It is important to note that Muslims do not believe that these patriarch-prophets all followed identical systems of worship and practice; rather, the prophets are all believed to have been exemplars of a more general *islām* in that each surrendered himself to the will and decree of God. In short, they are all understood to be "Muslims"—people who surrendered. Thus, we find in the Qur'ān two distinct meanings or usages of the term "islām": one universal and untied to a particular religious "law" or practice and one specific and tied directly to the belief system, law, and practice articulated by the Qur'ān and the historical life example of the prophet Muhammad.

As a particular religion beginning in the seventh century of the Common Era (CE), Islam includes both a basic belief system and a basic daily practice or discipline, and it includes something more: a radical change of perspective, a mental and attitudinal adjustment that seeks to envision and embrace every moment of one's life as an opportunity to surrender to the will and decree of the Divine. Thus, traditional Islam seeks to engage the person physically (in the daily acts of worship that are obligatory for all adult Muslims), rationally (in the few basic, nonnegotiable beliefs that all Muslims agree upon), and spiritually (in the way each soul is challenged to cultivate a transformative awareness of God's ever-presence). This last level of engagement can also be described as a sense of spiritual awareness that one is always in the presence of the Divine. We will explore this in much greater detail in the final chapter of this book.

According to a number of reliable chains of transmission,[1] one day, when the prophet Muhammad was sitting with some of his closest companions in the city of Yathrib (later to be known as "al-Medina"), a visitor came. He was dark-haired, garbed all in white, and he walked up to the Prophet with the standard greeting of peace (*"as-salāmu 'alaykum!"*). The Prophet returned his greeting and, much to the amazement of the companions, who did not know this newcomer, the visitor spoke with Muhammad in a most familiar fashion. First, he asked Muhammad to explain to him the meaning of belief or *"al-īmān,"* to which the Prophet replied that belief means believing in God, His angels, His books and messengers, Judgment Day, the ultimate meeting with God after death, and believing in God's providential determination of affairs, whether good or bad. "You are correct," the stranger replied. Then, the visitor asked the Prophet to explain to him the meaning of practice or *"al-islām,"* to which the Prophet replied that Islam is bearing witness that there is no God but God and that Muhammad is the messenger of God, offering regular prayers and paying the required charity for the needy, fasting the month of *Ramaḍān,* and—if one is able—making the pilgrimage to the house of God in Mecca if one can find a way. "You are correct," the stranger said again. Then he asked the Prophet to explain to him the meaning of righteousness or *"al-iḥsān,"* to which the Prophet replied that righteousness is worshiping God as if you see Him,

1. Including the *Ṣaḥīḥ* collections of both Muslim and Bukhārī.

and, failing to see God, it means worshiping God with the sure knowledge that God sees you.

The visitor left after a brief continuation of the discussion, and, after he went, Muhammad asked the companions present if they knew who that was. They said they had no idea. Then the Prophet told them that the visitor had been Gabriel, come to teach them about their religion.

An Overview of the Islamic Religious System

• The "Orthodoxy" of Islamic belief (*al-īmān*)—the rational *sacred worldview*

> God's Existence and Oneness
>
> The Angels
>
> The Books and the Messengers
>
> The Final Resurrection and the Day of Judgement
>
> God's Providence

• The "Orthopraxy" of Islam (*al-islām*)—the physical or embodied system of *sacred action*

> *The "Five Pillars" of Islamic devotional practice*
>
> > *Shahāda* (the act of testifying)
> >
> > *Ṣalāt* (ritual prayer observance)
> >
> > *Zakāt* (the purifying of wealth by tithing or alms tax)
> >
> > *Ṣawm/Ṣiyām* (fasting during the month of Ramaḍān)
> >
> > *Ḥajj* (making pilgrimage to Mecca once in one's lifetime, if possible)

• The foundation for spiritually-informed living (*al-iḥsān*)—the moral and attitudinal transformation that flows from the cultivated awareness of God's ever-presence, resulting in a *sacred disposition*

This "righteousness" represents the mental orientation that strives to place every moment of one's life in the presence of God, a transformative awareness unobstructed by ego, vain imaginings, preoccupations with the past or the future, worldly distractions, etc. *Al-iḥsān*, so understood, represents the core of Islam as both a religion and as a personal quest, for it focuses on the active surrender of the mind and heart, which is crucial for each believer's ultimate, and immanent, encounter with the Divine.

• Inner & Outer / Faith, Works, and Inner Disposition:

Some Qur'ānic passages pointing to the inseparable dimensions of a whole "Islamic" life

See, for example, "the Cow" / *al-baqara* (2):1–5, 152, 177; "Acts of Basic Assistance" / *al-māʿūn* (107); "the Fig" / *al-tīn* (95); 186; "the Family of ʿImrān" / *āl ʿimrān* (3):185–200.

• The Primary Sources for Islamic Theology and Life:

The *Qurʾān* (believed to be God's final revelation for humankind) and the *Sunnah* (custom/life-example) of God's final messenger, Muhammad, who is celebrated in the Qurʾān as the "beautiful role model" for Muslims (33:21) and as a man who was sent as "nothing but a mercy for the worlds" of God's creation (21:107).

~

Brief Note on the Qurʾān and the Prophetic Traditions

Literally "the recitation," the Qurʾān is believed to be the collection of more than twenty years of "recitations" revealed by God to the prophet Muhammad through the mediation of the archangel

Gabriel. Because of this composite or pieced together nature, the Qur'ān can be a most perplexing book to read. The revelations are not chronologically or even topically arranged, and so, at times, it seems to jump from topic to topic with no identifiable link or transition; at times, it refers to ancient peoples and prophets in the briefest of ways, as if its audience already knows these tales from start to finish; at other times, it unfolds continuous stories or narratives with almost biblical continuity (for example, see the twelfth *sūra* or chapter of Joseph). For these and other reasons, it stands apart as a unique sacred text.

However it may strike us, the Qur'ān is believed by Muslims to be the final revelation from God to humanity before Judgment Day. In its own perspective, it sees itself as a final and decisive articulation of the primordial religion ordained for humanity, the religion of Abraham and all the prophets. In the course of any responsible study, special attention must be paid to the context, content, organization, textual history, and interpretation of this "book" that is often called "God's Book" by believers.[2]

It is perhaps important to note at this introductory point that Muslims have traditionally drawn a very clear distinction between the Divine "voice" (i.e., the Qur'ānic recitations), and the human voice of the prophet Muhammad, whose words and deeds are recorded in separate collections, called "Ḥadīth" collections. Called the "beautiful role model" by the Qur'ān (33:21), the Prophet's life is seen as the exemplary standard for Muslims, and so these Ḥadīth works are essentially collections, usually arranged by subject, of "reports" (*aḥādīth*) concerning the way he lived as well as specific utterances, predictions, and admonitions he made. For most Muslims, these collections function as illustrations of Qur'ānic principles and helpful complements to the revelation, although some Muslims today go so far as to see the most reliable

---

2. There are many fine and widely available introductions to the Qur'ān in English. Two recent and very readable texts worthy of mention here are Farid Esack's *The Qur'an: A User's Guide* and Ingrid Mattson's *The Story of the Qur'an: Its History and Place in Muslim Life.*

traditions as being nearly equal to the revelation in their binding authority. Much more will be said about these traditions of the Prophet's life example in the course of our study.

3

Islam's Sacred Worldview, or Belief System

GOD

IF ONE were to ask a learned Muslim, "So, who or what is this God you worship?" the answers would never be able to capture the essence of the matter, for God (*Allāh* [i.e., *the* God]) in Islam is ultimately beyond (*akbar*) anything that can be thought or imagined. This affirmation of God's ultimate transcendence and unknowability is recalled many times every day in the Islamic call to prayer, which begins with the exclamation, "God is greater! God is greater!" ("*Allāhu akbar! Allāhu akbar!*").[1] This transcendent mystery called "God" can, however, be spoken of in terms of qualities or attributes or names, ninety-nine of which are explicitly identified in the Qur'ān.

> He is God, besides whom there is no god. He knows the un-
> seen and the visible, and he is ever Merciful, ever Gracious.
> He is God, besides whom there is no god. The Sovereign, the
> Holy, Peace, the ever-Faithful, the Protector, the Mighty, the
> All-Compelling, the Awe-Inspiring; Exalted is God above

---

1. According to one medieval Muslim authority, Abū Ḥāmid al-Ghazālī (from whom we will hear more later on in this book), this means that God's "greatness far exceeds all our powers of comprehension." See his *Alchemy of Happiness*, 22.

everything they associate with God. He is Allāh, the Creator, the Maker, the Fashioner. To Him belong the Most Beautiful Names; everything in the heavens and on the earth proclaims His glory, and He is the Mighty, the Wise. (the *sūra* of "the Gathering" [59]:22–24)

These attributes include titles such as "the One" (*al-ahad*), "the Merciful" (*al-rahmān*), "the Compassionate" (*al-rahīm*), "Truth" (*al-haqq*), "Peace" (*al-salām*), "the Judge of Judges" (*ahkam al-hākimīn*), "the Most Merciful of those who show mercy" (*arham al-rāhimīn*), "the Wise" (*al-hakīm*), "the Knowing" (*al-ʿalīm*), "the Powerful" (*al-qawī*), "the Ordainer" (*al-qadīr*), "the Forbearing" (*al-halīm*), "the Source of Right Guidance" (*al-hādī*), "the Light of the Heavens and the Earth" (*nūr al-samāwāt waʿl-ard*), and the like. While these names or qualities can shed some light on the "whoness" of the God pointed to by the Qurʾān, the whatness or the quiddity or essence of God remains forever a mystery, for—as the Qurʾān also says—"He has no partner" (6:163) and "there is nothing like unto Him" (42:11).

This God can also be spoken of historically as the God of the biblical prophets, including Adam, Noah, Lot, Abraham, Isaac, Jacob, Solomon, David, John the Baptist, and Jesus. In this way, Allāh is understood to be a God that intervenes in history and, through revelation to the prophets, instructs humanity in truths that would otherwise be unknowable.

> Recite!
> And your Lord is the most Generous,
> Who taught by means of the Pen,
> taught the human being that which he did not [previously] know. (the *sūra* of "the clot" [96]:3–5)

These truths, believed by Muslims to be the core of all of the divinely revealed religions, will be dealt with in this and subsequent chapters.

Here, in this brief and admittedly superficial discussion of the Infinite, it is crucial to add one more reflection. Immediately after affirming God's unity or singularity and God's lordship over everything, no Divine quality or characteristic should come before a clear and strong affirmation of Divine mercy, for everything, from the creation to revelation, flows from mercy. A moving example of this comes in the opening verses of the fifty-fifth *sūra* of the Qur'ān, a chapter called "the *sūra* of the Merciful."

> The Ever-Merciful!
> Who taught [humankind] the Qur'ān;
> Who created the human being;
> And taught him [the revelation] that makes everything clear:
> [how] the sun and the moon [move] in their calculated courses,
> [how] the stars and the trees prostrate themselves [before God],
> And [how] He raised the heavens and established the balance [for all things].
> So do not transgress the balance,
> And uphold the equilibrium with equity and justice, and do not corrupt the balance. (55:1–9)

If this is not sufficient as a word of comfort to believers, the Qur'ān also states in more than one passage that God has freely chosen to "write" or decree or legislate mercy upon Godself. No similar statement is made concerning any other attribute in the Qur'ān. For example, in *sūra(t) al-anām* ("the cattle," no. 6), we read, "Say: 'To whom belongs [all] that is in the heavens and on earth?' Say: 'to God, who has written upon Himself [the law of] mercy'" (6:12). Again, just a little later in the same *sūra*, we read,

> When those who believe in Our revelatory signs come to you, say: "Peace be upon you! Your Lord has written [the law of] mercy upon Himself so that if any of you commits evil out of ignorance and thereafter repents and reforms, [he shall realize that] God is ever-forgiving, full of mercy. (6:54)

At the risk of belaboring this point, as indeed the Qur'ān does, we read in *sūra(t) az-zumar* ("the group," no. 39), "Say: [God says] 'O My servants, who have transgressed against themselves! Do not give up on God's mercy! Verily God forgives all sins; indeed, He is the Ever-Forgiving, the Ever-Merciful."

Of course, this Qur'ānic emphasis upon Divine mercy does not mean that the Qur'ān and the prophetic traditions downplay Divine judgment and even Divine wrath upon those who knowingly oppress others and perpetrate evil on earth. On the contrary, the prophet Muhammad, like all the messengers of God, is believed to have been sent as both a herald of good news (*bashīr*) to the righteous and as a warner (*nadhīr*) to those who seek to falsify God's signs and do evil in the world. The promise and the threat are thus very central to the Qur'ānic moral teaching (as we will see below), but it cannot be overemphasized that these elements can only be understood within a wider theater of God's mercy. To clarify this point, one of the "sacred traditions" or theopathic utterances attributed to the prophet Muhammad (kept separate from the record of his personal sayings and doings as well as from the Qur'ānic recitations entrusted to him) puts these Divine words in the messenger's mouth: "My mercy prevails over My wrath."[2]

ANGELS

The Qur'ān posits an unseen realm that is densely populated and in continuous interaction with the visible world of humankind. Two kinds of sentient beings, in particular, are believed to animate the unseen worlds: the *jinn*, creatures created of fire and entrusted with free will[3] (similar in this regard to humans), and angels, creatures created of light and constantly occupied with the carrying out of God's will.

As we will hear much more about the *jinn* in the sixth chapter, just a few points will be noted here. According to the Qur'ān, some

2. Related from the Prophet by the companion Abū Hurayrah and recorded in the collections of al-Bukhārī, Muslim, Ibn Mājah and others. For a more detailed and eloquent description of the Qur'ānic conception of God, I urge readers to consult the first chapter of Fazlur Rahman's *Major Themes of the Qur'ān*.

3. This will seem less unfamiliar when we pause to recall that our English word, "genie," comes from this Arabic collective noun's singular version, "*jinnī*."

of the *jinn* are responsible for the evil "whisperings" or thoughts that occur to the human mind (see *sūra* 114). Others are virtuous and gather round whenever the Qur'ān is being chanted. They play far less a role in Islamic religious thought and in the daily lives of Muslims than they do in the storytelling traditions of classical Islam, but they are believed to be real and active inhabitants of the unseen dimensions of reality.

Angels are believed of a necessity, for they are understood to be the messengers through whom God "speaks" to prophets; such was the reported experience of the prophet Muhammad, who claimed regular visits from Gabriel for a period of twenty-three years. According to his accounts, these visits included conversation, personal instruction, and advice. More, angels are said to intervene and aid in human affairs whenever God commands it. Such was the case when the Prophet and his companions were facing their first battle in 624 CE against an overwhelmingly larger force; according to the Qur'ānic description of the event, angels were sent to fight alongside of the outnumbered Muslims, although the Muslims were unaware of it until later (see 3:125). In any event, the belief in angels is part of the nonnegotiable bedrock of Islamic belief, and so we find it mentioned in the above report, which indeed presents an angel as the prophet Muhammad's conversation partner.

THE BOOKS AND THE MESSENGERS

To be a Muslim means not to believe only in the Qur'ān and in the prophecy of Muhammad. Rather, it means to believe in the long tradition of prophets and messengers, some bearing "books" of revelation that included laws and spiritual instruction. Prophets of this latter kind are described as "messengers" and their number includes Moses (who is believed to have been given the Torah), David (who is believed to have been inspired to compose the Psalms), Jesus (whose revelation or "Gospel" seems to have included everything he said and taught), and Muhammad (who is believed to have received the Qur'ān by God through the mediation of the angel Gabriel). According to the Qur'ān, the essential message of all of the prophets is believed to be one and indivisible, but it is understood that unique laws and practices were given to each of them due to the unique needs and circumstances of their communities.

> Say: "We believe in God, and in that which has been sent down [i.e., revealed] to us, and in that which was revealed to Abraham and Ishmael and Isaac and Jacob and the Israelite tribes; and [we believe in] that which was given to Moses and Jesus and in what was given to the [other] prophets by their Lord. We make no distinction between any of them, and to God we surrender ourselves." (2:136)

Thus, while they are believed to be indivisible, no two prophets are quite the same, and each is considered according to his unique qualities, merits, and tasks. For example, Moses is said to have spoken to God directly, and Jesus is said to have been born of a virgin and to have had his full prophetic faculties at birth. More, Jesus is believed to be both the Jewish Messiah, although clearly understood here to be a specially anointed prophet but not in any sense part of the Divine essence, and a "word" (*kalimah*) of God:

> O people of the Book! Do not be excessive [or exceed the bounds of propriety] in your religion, and do not say anything of God except the truth. Verily, the Messiah—Jesus son of Mary—is the messenger of God and His word, which He spoke to Mary, and a spirit from Him." (4:171)

Jesus is also believed to be the prophet specially chosen to return near the End Times in order to defeat the Anti-Christ (*al-dajjāl*) and establish a period of peace and justice prior to the end of the world. Muhammad's primary distinction is that he came as the "seal" of the prophets, as the one sent to clarify and definitively restore the core prophetic message, and, in so doing, he is understood to be the last prophet (bringing the last divinely-revealed law [*sharī'ah*]) prior to the end of the world and the dawning of the Day of Judgment. Thus, when Jesus returns, Muslims believe that he will pray according to the Islamic practice (thus conforming to the most recent dispensation from God) and will lead an army of true believers in his campaign against the Anti-Christ.

THE LAST DAY AND THE "MEETING" WITH GOD

As has become clear, Islamic belief is built around the pious assumption that humanity originally came from God and to God every human being is returning. The idea of a final judgment, then, is universally accepted and enjoys much corroboration in both the Qur'ān and in the predictions and admonitions of the Prophet. Beyond judgment, Islamic belief includes a Heaven for the righteous and a Hell for the corrupt, although there has been much discussion through the centuries of whether Hell is a permanent state or whether it is more of a purgatorial place of suffering and purification prior to entering Paradise. The Qur'ānic accounts, when taken with the most reliable reports of the Prophet's teaching on this, seem to suggest that some will remain in the Fire forever while some will only be there for a time before eventually being brought into Paradise. As the pious Muslim interpreters of the Qur'ān always say, "God knows best."

GOD'S DETERMINATION OF AFFAIRS OR DIVINE PROVIDENCE

Many years ago when I was young and living in the West Bank near Bethlehem, there was an Arab bus that ran between Jerusalem and Bethlehem; I recall it was bus number 22. In any case, the very first time I flagged it down in Bethlehem with the intention of riding it to Jerusalem, I asked the driver (in what I later found out was ridiculously formal Arabic) if he was headed to Jerusalem. It must have sounded something like, "Peace be upon you! Whither art thou going, to Jerusalem?" The driver smiled, shrugged his shoulders, and said, "If God wills." For a moment, I froze, not knowing whether he was actually intending to go to Hebron, Ramallah, or another town; however, if God willed, he would unexpectedly end up in Jerusalem . . . After my moment of hesitation, I got on the bus, gave him the coin, and sat down, not knowing where we would end up. Of course, we went to Jerusalem, and thus began my education in the Islamic doctrine of Divine providence.

～

While it is believed by all Muslims that God is active in human history and that, ultimately, everything is within God's power and decree, the question of free will versus predestination remains a mystery. After the death of the Prophet, one of the first theological disagreements among the Muslims was over this question, and both sides found ample Qur'ānic and prophetic statements to support their claim. The debate was finally put to rest (to some extent) a few centuries later, when a widely-respected traditional theologian (Abū'l-Ḥasan al-Ashʿarī) unfolded a theory of "acquisition" (*kasb*), by which God was understood to be the Originator or the Creator of the deed while the human being was held responsible. In other words, the debate was put to rest by acknowledging the paradox: God is the only real "actor" or "creator" in the universe, and His power and knowledge envelop everything past, present, future; on the other hand, we feel as if we make choices, and we are promised reward and punishment based upon those choices.

For everyday purposes, pious Muslims live within this mystery. They worship and struggle to be virtuous as they ponder the Divine message hidden in the events of their days and of the larger, global situation. Perhaps the most tangible way this is perceived is through the pious phrase of exception, "if God wills" (*in shā 'Allāh*). Whenever a pious Muslim declares her attention to do something or to go somewhere, she says, "if God wills" as an acknowledgement that it may not come to pass even if she makes her best effort. In such cases, it is simply accepted as God's will, which is inscrutable and eternally beyond both human under-standing and human judgment.

⌇ *Questions for Reflection and Discussion*

1. In what ways is the Islamic belief system similar to that of other religions with which you are more familiar? In what ways does it seem unique, different, or foreign?

2. How do other monotheistic traditions resolve the question of God's omnipotence, omniscience, and providence, on the one hand, and human free will, on the other? For these traditions, can any event be outside the Divine plan? If the monotheistic God is a merciful God, as is so emphatically stressed in the Qur'ān, then how can tragedies (both natural and human-made) befall innocent people? Think; discuss.

Consider the following Qur'ānic passages:
   al-Raḥmān / "the Merciful" (55) and *al-Nahl* / "the Bees" (16)

3. What seems to be the Qur'ānic position on free will?

4. What are the "signs" of God referred to in these passages, and what is their overall significance for humanity?

Consider the following Qur'ānic passage:
   al-Kahf / "the Cave" (18):54–82

5. What is the "knowledge" Moses seeks in this passage?

6. How would you describe or characterize the Qur'ān's depiction of the relation between the visible and invisible "worlds"?

4

Islam's Path of Sacred Action (Obligatory Religious Practices)

IN ADDITION to being a religion built upon a few foundational, unchanging doctrines or rational assertions, Islam is a religion of obligatory practice and observance. I often explain this in terms of athletics, for the discipline of Islamic observance is easily understood when we think of it in athletic terms.

For example, if a person wants to run a marathon, we all understand that she will have to embrace a long-term, daily routine of training and discipline. This might include a special diet, a specific number of miles to run every day, a curbing or letting go of certain activities or behaviors that are not conducive for the training, and other life changes. While her work or study life might continue somewhat normally, everything else in her life, including her social life, would be touched and affected by the consuming preparations that are required for this great task.

In a sense, observant Muslims all see themselves as "in training" for a kind of marathon; the great task is making one's way home to God, in whose presence Muslims believe they will find their greatest happiness and peace. This worldly life is understood to be the training ground and the theater for the most crucial part of the race. Thus, the daily discipline an observant Muslim embraces is the basic part—the nuts and bolts—of the training, the preparation for the race into eternity. When seen in these terms, the daily prayer, the fasting, the almsgiving, the dietary observance, and the other aspects of Islamic practice may not seem so strange or foreign to us.

THE FIRST PILLAR

The Bearing Witness (*al-shahādah*)

The root meaning of the verb *shahida/yashhadu* in classical Arabic is "to witness" (something), to see or experience something firsthand, with one's own eyes. By extension, then, it has been used as the standard expression for testifying in court and witnessing an official event (such as the signing of a document or the completion of a legal transaction). The verbal noun, which can be translated as "the act of bearing witness," also carries a religious meaning and stands as the determining factor for officially considering a person "Muslim."

Since the time of the Prophet, the gateway to Islam has been the public utterance or testimony that "there is no god but God, and Muhammad is the messenger of God." Said in front of at least two reliable Muslim witnesses to be accepted by the Muslim community, this utterance sums up what it has traditionally meant to be a Muslim: acknowledging no power worthy of reliance and worship save God's power and accepting the authority of the "final" message entrusted to the prophet Muhammad. While these two parts of the pronouncement are found nowhere thus connected in the Qur'ān, each is found separately in its verses, and so the formula is regarded as unquestionably authentic.

It is important to remember that, in the first days of the movement, such a pronouncement came at a terrific cost. It meant taking a clear stand even when it could mean being cut off from your family, shamed, or even being persecuted for your public allegiance (we will treat this more fully in chapter 6). Indeed, for many Muslim converts in the West today, publicly "coming out" as a Muslim can have similar repercussions. The *shahādah* thus has a significance that goes beyond a private belief in one's heart; it means rejecting all other lords and taking a public stand that God is the One and only God. To some extent, the public nature of this pillar speaks of a life commitment to a distinct way of living, and so it has been understood over the centuries. Witnessing becomes the very essence of faithful living, an act performed not once but over and over again every minute of a Muslim's life.

> And so We have made you to be a community of the middle way, so that you might be witness bearers unto the people, and so that the Messenger [Muhammad] might be a witness unto you. (2:143)

THE SECOND PILLAR

THE RITUAL PRAYER (*al-ṣalāh*)

During another visit to the Middle East in the winter and spring of 1986, I found myself in East Jerusalem and badly in need of a haircut. I found a barber shop off of Salāḥ al-Dīn Street, walked in and asked the barber if he would cut my hair. He agreed, and I sat right down.

About halfway into the haircut, the mid-afternoon call to prayer came:

> *God is greater! God is greater!*
> *I bear witness that there is no god but God!*
> *I bear witness that there is no god but God!*
> *I bear witness that Muhammad is the messenger of God!*
> *I bear witness that Muhammad is the messenger of God!*
> *Come to prayer! Come to prayer!*
> *Come to prosperity! Come to prosperity!*
> *God is greater! God is greater!*
> *There is no god but God!*

The chant cut through the warm afternoon air . . . I had been residing in Bethlehem for a few months at this point, and the call had become a familiar and anticipated marker in the various stages of my days. What followed on this particular afternoon, however, surprised me a little.

Without a word of explanation or apology, the barber abandoned the project of my haircut. His son brought me a cup of hot tea (with a healthy amount of sugar already added), and the barber went to the sink, where he began to wash. First, he washed his hands and face a few times; then, it seemed he was rinsing out his nostrils and his mouth. After this, with face dripping, he washed his forearms carefully up to the elbows. Dripping now from his chin and arms, he ran wet hands over his head and wiped the back of his neck. Then, finally, he lifted his right foot and rinsed it thoroughly under the tap. He did the same with his left, and, with that, he finally reached for a towel and quickly dabbed his hands and face.

Next, he took out a small carpet and unrolled it on the floor. He did this at a precise angle, and so it seemed the direction was important. Then, still without a word of explanation to me, he began to silently recite the prayer. Four times he stood and bowed, straightened and fell to his hands and knees with forehead on the ground. Careful not to make a noise, I sipped my tea and watched in wonder.

After a few minutes, it was all over. Still without a word of apology for the delay in my haircut or a word of explanation, he walked over, gently smiled, and lifted the empty teacup out of my hands. He then resumed the haircut, and I was struck by the way all this had unfolded. It was natural, organic, and needed no explanation. Prayer for him seemed like breathing itself; the only difference I could discern was the fact that one was involuntary and the other was voluntary. His manner, however, suggested to me that, for him, the prayer had crossed over and had become more than a chosen practice or even a habit; it had become a vital function.

More than a dozen centuries before this event, the Prophet is reported to have been with his companions in Medina. According to the tradition, he asked his companions, "If there was a river flowing outside your house and you washed in it five times every day, would you ever be dirty?" They answered, "No." He concluded, "That's what prayer is."

∽

The prayer in Islam is considered to be the most important practice, for it serves as a comprehensive "call" to come back to a God-centered awareness at several key points in the day: predawn, noon, mid afternoon, sunset, and night. Each prayer consists of two or more "cycles" of prostrations and recitations, and, in each cycle, the first chapter of the Qur'ān is recited:

> In the name of God, the Merciful, the Beneficent.
>
> All praise be to God, the Lord of the worlds,
>
> The Merciful, the Beneficent,
>
> Master of the Day of Judgment.
>
> You are the One whom we worship, and to You do we fly for help; Guide us along the straight path, the path of those whom You bless, not [the path of] those who incur anger, nor the path of those who wander, lost.

This is a prayer for guidance, a prayer that first clarifies the One to whom the prayer is addressed and why; it is a prayer by which the Muslim begs to be guided and thus spared from being counted among those who know better and yet do wrong ("those who incur anger") and from being counted among those who lack a sense of purpose and do not know the difference between right and wrong ("those who wander" or "stray"). It is also a prayer that reminds the supplicant of death and judgment, crucial principles for the prioritization of one's worldly affairs. In essence, then, the prayer can be seen as an ongoing and oft-repeated reminder to the Muslim, a reminder of the reality of God, God's existence and oneness, a reminder of death and judgment, a reminder of the need for God's mercy and guidance. This reminder comes to call the

Muslim back to herself and to what is believed to be her highest happiness and well-being. "Come to prayer," the call to prayer recites; "come to prosperity."

We will delve more deeply into the practice and meaning of prayer later on in the book, but even with this simple introduction, one can see the power this ritual can have in a person's life.

THE THIRD PILLAR

THE CHARITY TAX (*al-zakāh*)

While there are some variations among the various schools of Islamic jurisprudence, al-*zakāh* or *al-zakāt* is a religious tax of approximately 2.5 percent of a Muslim's annually accrued wealth left over after basic expenses have been paid and the needs of the family have been met. The *zakāt* funds, once collected by an official government agency or by a local mosque or charity, are then to be redistributed among the needy (including the impoverished, refugees, those enslaved to debt, those simply enslaved) or spent on public, philanthropic projects that will benefit everyone, such as the building of public hospitals, the establishment of philanthropic endowments, and the like.

The word for the charity tax, *al-zakāt*, comes from a verbal root whose meaning is "to thrive" or "to be pure." Muslim scholars thus argue that this religious obligation seeks to purify the individual from his or her own greed by forcing them to give a portion of their income to the needy; it further seeks to purify the heart of the poor or disadvantaged person from the envy they would otherwise feel were they not the recipients of this charity; and finally it seeks to purify the society by lessening the extreme imbalance of wealth and poverty. Whatever its ultimate effects, it reflects a kind of social welfare principle that places a responsibility upon "those who have" to care for "those who have not." While the society of Medina during the Prophet's final ten years may not have been the first society to have instituted such a system, it stands as a fourteen-hundred-year-old attempt to combat poverty and to lessen the gap between the wealthiest and the most impoverished sectors of society.

THE FOURTH PILLAR

FASTING THE MONTH OF RAMADĀN (*al-ṣawm/al-ṣiyām*)

Stressing the continuity of this practice through the Judaic and Christian revelations, the Qur'ān simply says that "Fasting is prescribed for you, just as it was prescribed for those who came before" (2:183). There is strong evidence to suggest that, prior to the "coming down" of this verse, the prophet Muhammad observed the Jewish fast of Yom Kippur (the Day of Atonement), known as the "tenth" (*'āshūrā*) of the month of Tishri in the pre-Islamic calendar.[1] Once the verse above was "sent down" in Medina, the new month-long fast was instituted, making the fast of *'āshūrā* optional. So it has been observed ever since.

During Ramaḍān, all able-bodied, adult Muslims are required to observe a total fast (no food, water, sexual activity, or smoking) during the daylight hours, stretching from the predawn daylight to sunset. As they struggle with the hunger and thirst, they are encouraged to struggle with any and all aspects of their character that are morally rebellious and not in a state of harmony with or surrender to God's law. Fasting thus is seen as a vehicle for purification and spiritual advancement, a practice that reestablishes the supremacy of mind over body, and it is also seen as a practice that opens one's heart more fully to the suffering of others. In particular, then, Ramaḍān is also meant to be a month of charity and

1. See Peters, *Muhammad and the Origins of Islam*, 215–16. It is important here to note that the Islamic calendar, which is strictly lunar (new moon to new moon), modified the pre-Islamic calendar, which had extra, intercalary days inserted to keep it stable within the longer, solar year, and so the optional fast of *'āshūrā* no longer falls upon the day of Yom Kippur in the Jewish calendar.

outreach to those who fast not by choice but are forced to do so by the cruelty of their impoverished situations.

Far from being a month dreaded by the faithful, Ramaḍān is a month that Muslims are brought-up to love and to which they look forward. The evenings of this special month are filled with special foods and family gatherings, visits between relatives and friends, special night prayers and vigils at the mosques, etc. The mood is thus generally festive and hopeful, and people often emerge from the month with a sense of renewal and new possibility.

THE FIFTH PILLAR

THE PILGRIMAGE TO THE HOUSE (al-Ḥajj)

Once in one's lifetime, if it can be afforded, every Muslim is required to make a journey to Mecca during the specially-appointed days of pilgrimage, when millions of Muslims from all over the world gather to observe ancient rites as they pray for God's forgiveness and blessing.

Islam is a religion that is built upon the notion of journeying, making one's way through this world and back "home" to God. For example, Islam—as a formal religion and comprehensive way of life—really began in the year that Muhammad and his companions made a journey, the *hijrah* or "migration," to the refuge of Yathrib, later to be called al-Madīna, where they could live free from persecution and begin building a community. For Muslims, this migration symbolizes any movement from persecution to freedom, from sin to virtue, from ignorance to knowledge. Much more will be said about this historic migration and its expanded significance in chapter 8.

The journey motif touches almost every aspect of the Muslim's life. Another example comes in the Islamic code of ideal living, the *sharī'ah*. The word comes from an old desert word that describes the trampled path that leads to an oasis or water hole. By extension, then, the *sharī'ah* is the way that leads to water, to life, and to the refreshment of the whole person. It is the way walked by others before and the way that others will walk after us. Indeed, this way is the very essence of religious conduct, and every community is believed to have been shown such a path through the revelation bestowed upon its messenger—one of their own who related God's signs to them in their own language and in a way that made sense given their own culture and circumstances.

> We have appointed a [unique] law (*shir'ah*) and way of life (*minhāj*) for each of you. If God had so willed, He could have made you a single community; however, [He did otherwise] in order to test you by means of what He has given you. Therefore, vie with one another in the race to do good works! Unto God you are all returning, and so He will make clear to you [then] that in which you have differed. (5:48)

According to the specificities of the Islamic *sharī'ah*, this path or way of life includes a command to make a journey to God's "house" in Mecca, where—at least according to the Qur'ān—Abraham and his son Ishmael erected the first temple or "house" for the worshiping of one God.[2] And so, for a Muslim to celebrate the pilgrimage is to commemorate Abraham's journey from his home in Mesopotamia to the west, where he made his home and fathered two sons, Ishmael and Isaac. To celebrate the pilgrimage is to commemorate the journey of Ishmael and his mother, Hagar, into the desert wilderness where they miraculously found water in the form of a well/spring that gushed out of the arid, rocky ground when Hagar had given up all hope of life. This frantic search is reenacted by the pilgrims in their performance of the *sa'ī*, one of the pilgrimage rites that involves the running between two hills near the well of Zamzam in Mecca.

As a practical act and pillar of Islam, the pilgrimage is full of ancient and often perplexing actions, some of which may strike

---

2. See al-Qur'ān 3:96–97. This is treated with much more detail in chapter 5.

us as curious and others as bewildering. It is important to stress, however, that the experience of the pilgrimage is itself a journey, and no pilgrim's experience of the rites is ever separate from the journey.

In Arabic, the word for pilgrimage (*ḥajj*) is related to the word for "proof" (*ḥujjah*). Contemplating this connection, Muslim masters speak of the life-change that comes when one completes the journey. Pilgrims are meant to return reborn, with a certitude and commitment that they did not know before. We witness this in the conversations we have with those who have gone, in the testimonials we read from those who have made the journey and completed the ancient rites. They may put on their old clothes when they have finished, but many claim that these clothes belonged to someone else, to someone they used to be prior to the experience.

One such example comes in the autobiography of Malcolm X, whose life changed dramatically when he went on the *ḥajj*. Without a doubt, his journey to Mecca remains one of the most treasured and influential American Islamic stories. As soon as he had completed the rites of pilgrimage, Malcolm started writing letters to his family and friends in America. "Here is what I wrote," he recorded, "from my heart."

> Never have I witnessed such sincere hospitality and the overwhelming spirit of true brotherhood as is practiced by people of all colors and races here in this Ancient Holy Land, the home of Abraham, Muhammad, and all the other prophets of the Holy Scriptures. For the past week, I have been utterly speechless and spellbound by the graciousness I see displayed all around me by people of all colors.

> I have been blessed to visit the holy city of Mecca. I have made my seven circuits around the Ka'ba, led by a young *Mutawaf* named Muhammad. I drank water from the well of ZemZem. I ran seven times back and forth between the hills of Mt. Al-Safa and Al-Marwah. I have prayed in the ancient city of Mina, and I have prayed on Mt. Arafat.

There were tens of thousands of pilgrims, from all over the world. They were of all colors, from blue-eyed blonds to black-skinned Africans. But we were all participating in the same ritual, displaying a spirit of unity and brotherhood that my experiences in America had led me to believe could never exist between the white and the non-white.

America needs to understand Islam, because this is the one religion that erases from its society the race problem. Throughout my travels in the Muslim world, I have met, talked to, and even eaten with people who in America would have been considered "white"—but the "white" attitude was removed from their minds by the religion of Islam. I have never before seen sincere and true brotherhood practiced by all colors together, irrespective of their color.

You may be shocked by these words coming from me. But on this pilgrimage, what I have seen, and experienced, has forced me to rearrange much of my thought-patterns previously held, and to toss aside some of my previous conclusions . . .

During the past eleven days here in the Muslim world, I have eaten from the same plate, drunk from the same glass, and slept in the same bed (or on the same rug)—while praying to the same God—with fellow Muslims, whose eyes were the bluest of blue, whose hair was the blondest of blond, and whose skin was the whitest of white. And in the words and in the actions and in the deeds of the "white" Muslims, I felt the same sincerity that I felt among the black African Muslims of Nigeria, Sudan, and Ghana.

We were truly all the same (brothers)—because their belief in one God had removed the "white" from their minds, the "white" from their behavior, and the "white" from their attitude.[3]

Thus we see how, while the rituals themselves are an integral part of the *hajj*, often the journey itself proves to be the most

3. As told to Alex Haley in his *Autobiography of Malcolm X*, 346–47.

transformative aspect of this fifth and final "pillar" of the faith. Malcolm X's beautiful and inspiring words attest to this, even as they call out a challenge to many Muslim societies, where numerous forms of ethnic and religious and gender-based discrimination continue. Malcolm's moving yet almost romantic glimpse of the Islamic ideal sadly clashes with many Muslim realities, and so his proposed remedy for America (i.e., the spiritual egalitarianism of Islam) can and should be seen as the remedy for many "Muslim" societies as well.

A Word on the Historical Evolution of the Islamic Religious Sciences and the Rise of "Sufism" as a Religious Science

In the centuries that witnessed the dawn of Islam, the expansion of its empire and its first intellectual florescence, the majority of the intellectual zeal—at least among the ranks of the pious—was devoted to the most essential, immediate needs, such as the basic systematization and codification of the new religion. Thus, the early scholars (*'ulamā'*) began specializing in obvious areas that had practical applications in people's daily lives, areas such as Arabic grammar and the proper methods for reciting and interpreting the Qur'ān,[4] the gathering and verification of the reports of the Prophet's precedent-setting words and deeds,[5] the "understanding" and codification of the Islamic way of life based on the *sharī'ah*,[6] an ideal code of divinely-ordained conduct embedded within the sacred texts and prophetic traditions, and also the assembling of the *'aqīdah* or creed (i.e., the scholarly authorization of the non-negotiable beliefs required of anyone calling themselves a "Muslim"). Intertwined with the codification of the creed was a

4. Collectively grouped within the standard heading of "the Qur'ānic Sciences," or *'ulūm al-Qur'ān*.

5. Collectively grouped under the heading of "the Sciences of Ḥadīth," or *'ulūm al-ḥadīth*.

6. Known as the science of "Islamic Law/Jurisprudence," or *al-fiqh*.

science of dogmatic theology (*al-kalām*)[7] that relied upon logic and dialectical argumentation as it sought to clarify, explain, systematize and defend the basic creed against "heretical" innovations.

In other words, establishing the specifics of the orthopraxy (*al-islām*) and the orthodoxy (*al-īmān*) consumed the attention of the vast majority of religious scholars in the first centuries of the faith. While this process unfolded, the military and political successes of the first century necessitated that the government (i.e., the "caliphate") devote most of its attention to the consolidation of power and the administration of the increasingly vast and complex empire.[8] Some Muslims, however, sensing a danger in this focus upon political matters and the external requirements of the faith, began to elucidate and codify a religious science that focused on the inner life (*al-iḥsān*), a science also rooted in the Qur'ān, the prophetic custom, and the practice of the closest companions. This was called by some scholars and practitioners the "Science of the Way of the Afterlife" (*'ilm ṭarīq al-ākhira*), although the name that came to stick was "Sufism" (*al-taṣawwuf*), and it included both a practical, action-oriented knowledge that concerned the purification of the heart and a theoretical dimension that entered into the mysteries of faith.

Acknowledging the ongoing validity and necessity of the duty or action-oriented religious science of "right practice" or jurisprudence (*al-fiqh*), these scholar-practitioners of the inner way argued that external form was not enough as they turned their attention to the scrutiny of inner acts (i.e., to the study of the attitudes, intentions, and mental states that are essential for the purification

---

7. Both speculative and scholastic, *kalām* is a very difficult phenomenon/movement to translate. "Dogmatic theology" strikes us as the most appropriate rendering due to the fact that, generally speaking, these "theologians" (*mutakallimūn*) took the revelation as their starting point and used reason to explain and vigorously defend it, thus constructing a worldview to accommodate it.

8. For a brief summary of this early formation of the tradition, see Majid Fakhry's *History of Islamic Philosophy*, xvii–xxii.

and governance of hearts striving to make their way toward God). Thus the sphere in which these spiritual masters or "Scholars of the Afterlife" ('ulamā' al-ākhirah) exercised their judgment and authority was the unseen world of the heart, a subtle domain beyond the perception of physical eyes and yet perceivable through experience and the spiritual eye of intuitive understanding.

In the final chapter of this small book, we will examine this area of mystical spirituality in greater detail and depth. For now, let it suffice that we see early Islam emerging as a way of life that includes one's physical practice and way of life (al-islām), one's rational worldview (al-īmān), and one's more mystical and intimate connection with the Divine (al-iḥsān). In short, Islam represents an attempt to reorient or redesign one's entire person and cultural life in a theocentric or "God-centered" way, and, in so doing, it does indeed resemble the fundamental aspiration of those choosing a monastic life within the Christian context. So sometimes our first impressions reflect an enduring ray of truth.

~ *Questions for Reflection and Discussion*

1. Islam is sometimes described as an "orthopraxy" or as a religion that emphasizes ritual and obligatory practice above belief and spirituality. Based on your readings, observations, and real-world interactions with Muslims, does this sound accurate or fair to you? What is the place of the physical practice and ritual observance in Islam? In other faiths? What is the relation of ritual and embodied practice to the less observable, more personal dimensions of faith and spirituality? Can one exist fully without the other?

2. Does the Islamic conception of God allow for a deity that derives benefit from the acts performed by worshipers? If not for the appeasement or benefit of God, why then might such acts of worship be required of Muslim men and women? Read and discuss sūrah 29.

SECTION III

History

And so the pair set off until they encountered a young man; when they encountered him, [the guide] killed him. [Moses] said, "You have killed an innocent soul without [the death of another] soul [upon him]? You have done something detestable!"

[The guide] replied, "Did I not tell you that you would be unable to hold patience with me?"

[Moses] said, "If I question you about anything after [this], then do not take me as your companion! For you will have won a [solid] excuse from me."

And so the two proceeded . . . when they came to the people of a village, they asked for food, but they [i.e., the inhabitants] refused to treat them [properly] as guests. So the pair found there a wall that was on the point of collapsing. [The guide] then raised it up straight. [Moses] said: "If you had wished, surely thou could have taken some payment for [doing] that!"

[The guide] then said, "This is the moment of parting between me and you: [But first] I shall reveal to you the true interpretation (al-taʾwīl) of that concerning which you were unable to hold patience.

~ The Qurʾān, from the *sūra* of the Cave / *al-kahf* (18):74–78

5

The Eastern Branch of the Abrahamic Covenant

Ishmael, the Ka'ba, and the Mythic History of Arabia Prior to the Rise of Islam

And whosoever dislikes and turns away from the religious way of Abraham has foolishly debased himself; for We deemed him pure and favored him in this world, and surely, in the Hereafter, he is among the righteous.

    ❧ The Qur'ān, from the *sūra* of "the Cow" / "*al-baqara*" (2):130

OFTEN, WHEN I begin discussing Islam's understanding of its own origins, I turn to a source that, for some students, seems surprising: the Hebrew Bible, called by Christians the "Old Testament." Here, in the very first of the books attributed to Moses, we find a story that has everything to do with the beginnings of Islam. This is the story of Abram, the Mesopotamian who, upon entering into a covenant with Yahweh, became known forever after as Abraham, the father of monotheism and the traditions of Judaism, Christianity, and Islam.

In the events leading up to the pact or covenant between Abram and God, Abram had turned away from the polytheism of his father in Mesopotamia (modern-day Iraq) and had journeyed southwest into the lands of the Philistines and the Canaanites (modern-day Israel and the Palestinian territory of the West Bank). There, Abram became wealthy, with many flocks and servants, but he had no children. His wife, Sarai, was unable to conceive a child, and so she offered her servant maiden, an Egyptian girl named Hagar (in Hebrew, literally "the stranger"), to her husband as a surrogate or "stand in" wife. We can imagine that such arrangements were probably somewhat common in a culture that held the bearing of children to be the main function of a wife. Sarai herself says to her husband in Genesis, "Look, the Lord has kept me from bearing. Consort with my maid; perhaps I shall have a son through her" (Gen 16:2).

In any case, as the biblical story goes, Hagar came to occupy the position of concubine or second wife to Abram, and she conceived. The Bible suggests that her success in conceiving a child gave her a reason to look down upon Sarai, her mistress, who had never been able to conceive. Hagar's "uppity" attitude was more than Sarai could bear. Sarai thus pulled rank and used it to put the younger woman in her place. As the Hebrew Bible relates the story,

> And Sarai said to Abram, "The wrong done me is your fault! I myself put my maid in your bosom; now that she is pregnant, I am lowered in her esteem. The Lord decide between you and me!" Abram said to Sarai, "Your maid is in your hands. Deal with her as you think right." Then Sarai treated her harshly, and she ran away from her.
>
> An angel of the Lord found her by a spring of water in the wilderness, the spring on the road to Shur, and said, "Hagar, slave of Sarai, where have you come from, and where are you going?" And she said, "I am running away from my mistress, Sarai."

> And the angel of the Lord said to her, "Go back to your mistress, and submit to her harsh treatment." And the angel of the Lord said to her,
>
> "I will greatly increase your offspring, and they shall be too many to count."
>
> And the angel of the Lord said to her further, "Behold, you are with child and shall bear a son; You shall call him Ishmael, for the Lord has paid heed to your suffering. He shall be a wild ass of a man; His hand against everyone, and everyone's hand against him; He shall dwell alongside all of his kinsmen."
>
> . . . Hagar bore a son to Abram, and Abram gave the son that Hagar bore the name Ishmael. Abram was eighty-six years old when Hagar bore Ishmael to Abram. (Gen 16:5–16)

And so a son was born to Abram, a son whose name literally means "God hears" or "God heard," for God heeded the suffering of his mother, Hagar. For a number of years, Ishmael was the only son of his father, and we can easily glean from the Genesis account that he was very dear to his father, for in traditional societies the birth of a son is treated as the real continuation and fulfillment of the father's legacy. More, when there are multiple sons, the elder son is traditionally awarded more honor and responsibility.

Thirteen years later, a day came when God summoned Abram and formally established his covenant with him. Abram's name was changed to Abraham, which means "father of a multitude," and Abraham sealed his part of the bargain through his own circumcision and the circumcision of all the male members of his household. The Bible recounts that Ishmael was with him and was initiated by his father into the pact with God, an agreement that was to include all of their offspring in perpetuity.

> When Abram was ninety-nine years old, the Lord appeared to Abram and said to him, "I am El Shaddai. Walk in my ways and be blameless. I will establish My covenant between Me and you, and I will make you exceedingly numerous."

> Abram threw himself on his face; and God spoke to him further, "As for Me, this is My covenant with you: You shall be the father of a multitude of nations. And you shall no longer be called Abram, but your name shall be Abraham, for I make you the father of a multitude of nations. I will make you exceedingly fertile, and make nations of you; and kings shall come forth from you. I will maintain My covenant between Me and you, and your offspring to come, as an everlasting covenant throughout the ages, to be God to you and to your offspring to come. I assign the land you sojourn in to you and your offspring to come, all the land of Canaan, as an everlasting holding. I will be their God."

> God said further to Abraham, "As for you, you and your offspring to come throughout the ages shall keep My covenant. Such shall be the covenant between Me and you and your offspring to follow which you shall keep: every male among you shall be circumcised. You shall circumcise the flesh of your foreskin, and that shall be the sign of the covenant between Me and you. And throughout the generations, every male among you shall be circumcised at the age of eight days. As for the homeborn slave and the one bought from an outsider who is not of your offspring, they must be circumcised, homeborn, and purchased alike. Thus shall My covenant be marked in your flesh as an everlasting pact." (Gen 17:1–13)

As a blessing and sign of God's favor for his servant Abraham, God caused Abraham's wife, Sarai, to conceive in her old age. Thus we have the emergence of Isaac, the second son and the one through whom the line of the Hebrew patriarchs would be passed down.

> And God said to Abraham, "As for your wife Sarai, you shall not call her Sarai, but her name shall be Sarah. I will bless her; indeed, I will give you a son by her. I will bless her so that she will give rise to nations; rulers of peoples shall issue from her." Abraham threw himself on his face and laughed, as he said to himself, "Can a child be born to a man a hundred years old, or can Sarah bear a child at ninety?" And Abraham said to God, "O that Ishmael might live by your favor!" God said, "Nevertheless, Sarah your wife shall bear you a son, and you

shall name him Isaac; and I will maintain my covenant with
him as an everlasting covenant for his offspring to come. As
for Ishmael, I have heeded you. I hereby bless him. I will make
him fertile and exceedingly numerous. He shall be the father
of twelve chieftains, and I will make of him a great nation.
But my covenant I will maintain with Isaac, whom Sarah shall
bear to you at this season next year." And when He was done
speaking with him, God was gone from Abraham.

Then Abraham took his son Ishmael, and all his homeborn
slaves and all those he had bought, every male in Abraham's
household, and he circumcised the flesh of their foreskins
on that very day, as God had spoken to him. Abraham was
ninety-nine years old when he circumcised the flesh of his
foreskin, and his son Ishmael was thirteen years old when he
was circumcised in the flesh of his foreskin. Thus Abraham
and his son Ishmael were circumcised on that very day; and
all his household, his homeborn slaves and those that had
been bought from outsiders, were circumcised with him.
(Gen 17:15–27)

As the Bible tells the unfolding story, Sarah does indeed
give birth to a son named Isaac, and, one day as she was watch-
ing her son playing with his elder brother Ishmael, she became
jealous and told her husband to cast out Ishmael and his mother.
Understandably, this caused Abraham great disturbance and inter-
nal conflict, but God spoke to him, reassured him, and instructed
him to proceed with the banishment of the slave concubine and
her son.

But God said to Abraham, "Do not be distressed over the boy
of your slave; whatever Sarah tells you do as she says, for it is
through Isaac that offspring shall be continued for you. As for
the son of the slave woman, I will make a nation of him, too,
for he is your seed."

Early next morning Abraham took some bread and a skin
of water, and gave them to Hagar. He placed them over her
shoulder, together with the child, and sent her away. And she
wandered about in the wilderness of Beer-sheba. When the

water was gone from the skin, she left the child under one of the bushes, and went and sat down at a distance, a bowshot away; for she thought, "Let me not look on as the child dies." And sitting thus afar, she burst into tears.

God heard the cry of the boy, and an angel of God called to Hagar from heaven and said to her. "What troubles you, Hagar? Fear not, for God has heeded the cry of the boy where he is. Come, lift up the boy and hold him by the hand, for I will make a great nation of him." Then God opened her eyes and she saw a well of water. She went and filled the skin with water, and let the boy drink. God was with the boy and he grew up; he dwelt in the wilderness and became a bowman. He lived in the wilderness of Paran; and his mother got a wife for him from the land of Egypt. (Gen 21:12–21)

Thus, Ishmael and his mother eventually settled in the wilderness of "Paran" to the southeast. There they wandered until, deep into the desert, they ran out of water. In spite of Hagar's frantic search for water, they found none, and Hagar began to despair. But "God heard" ("Ishmael") the cries of the boy, and miraculously a well appeared. There, in the vicinity of that well, Hagar and Ishmael settled, Genesis 21 relates, and there Ishmael married to become himself the father of a great nation foretold by God. Genesis 25 goes on to name each of Ishmael's twelve sons.

We don't see much of Ishmael after this in Genesis, but he does come into the story at least once more, when his father Abraham dies. According to the biblical account in Genesis 25, Abraham was buried by both of his sons, Isaac and Ishmael, and this is interesting, for it acknowledges some ongoing contact and collaboration between the two branches of Abraham's family, at least up to his death.

Now, while scholars continue to debate and question the exact historicity of these Bible stories, what is important for us to note here is the fact that this story serves as a foundation for the subsequent development of Judaic, Christian, and Islamic origins.

In fact, rather than contradicting the biblical story of Abraham, the Qur'ān continues and expands it.

The Qur'ānic expansion of the story places Abraham with Ishmael and Hagar in the desert, where he apparently found them living near the well mentioned in the biblical text. Here, in addition to helping them get settled, he is reported to have instructed his son in the ways of monotheistic worship. Together, they are reported to have erected a shrine or "house" for the worship of God, and, forever after, the shrine and the well were bound to the Abraham story in the desert. A town grew around the well and shrine, and this town came to be called "Makka" (Mecca), a few hundred miles southeast of the biblical encampment of Abraham in Beer-sheba.

> And [remember] when Abraham was tested by his Lord with certain commands, which he fulfilled. He [God] said, "Verily, I am making you a leader/patriarch for the people." He [Abraham] said, "And of my progeny." He [God] said, "[but] My covenant will not reach those who do evil."

> And [remember] when We made the House a place of gathering and safety for the people. So take the standing place of Abraham as a place of prayer. We made our covenant with Abraham and Ishmael in order that they sanctify my House for those who walk round it, use it as a retreat, and bow down in prostration.[1]

> And [remember] when Abraham said, "My Lord! Make this a city of peace, and provide fruits for its people, those who believe in God and the Last Day. He [God] replied, "And, as for those who ungratefully reject faith, I will afford them a

1. This refers to the ritual act of circumambulation, literally "going around" (*ṭawāf*) the cube-shaped shrine of the Kaʿba. When Muslims visit the shrine, they traditionally walk round it in a counterclockwise direction seven times, all the while praising God, seeking God's forgiveness, asking for blessings upon themselves, upon the prophet Muhammad, and remembering Abraham. Many masters of Islamic spiritual traditions have said that this circumambulation of the Kaʿba on earth mirrors the circling of God's Throne in the next world. The Kaʿba thus represents the earthly equivalent of God's throne.

pleasant life for a little while, then I will drive them into the torment of the fire and a wretched end."

And [remember] when Abraham and Ishmael raised the foundations of the House [and prayed], "Our Lord! Accept [this act] from us! Surely You are the Hearing, the Knowing!

"Our Lord! Make of us people who have surrendered to you, and [make] of our descendants a nation that has wholly surrendered to you! And show us the places for [the celebration] of rites, and turn to use in mercy, for verily You are the One Oft Returning [to us], Full of Mercy.

"Our Lord! Send in their midst a Messenger, one of their own who will recite Your signs to them and teach them the Book and the Wisdom, one who will purify them. Verily, You are the Mighty, the Wise!"

And whosoever dislikes and turns away from the religious way of Abraham has foolishly debased himself; for We deemed him pure and favored him in this world, and surely, in the Hereafter, he is among the righteous. (from the *sūra* of "the Cow" / *al-baqara* [2]:124–30)

The primary reason why Muslims revere the site of the Ka'ba, then, is their belief that it is the oldest monotheistic shrine on the planet, the shrine built by Abraham himself, with the help of his elder son Ishmael. Whatever one believes about the historicity of this story, the shrine of the Ka'ba and the spring of Zamzam flowing beside it together formed the heart of the western Arabian town of Mecca, which was—even from ancient times, long before the coming of the prophet Muhammad—associated with the story of Abraham, Ishmael, and Hagar.

The Qur'ān clearly echoes the Hebrew Bible in announcing the good news of Sarah's pregnancy with Isaac (11:69–73) and acknowledges that the main branch of the covenant continued through the bloodline of Isaac, Jacob ("Israel"), and the twelve sons of Jacob, but we also find that the Qur'ān, similar to the Hebrew Bible, asserts that the covenant had another branch that was transplanted in the wilderness, where it took root and became a great nation in its own right. And so we see the rise of the biblical "Ishmaelites"—the Arabs—who gradually slip out of the biblical picture, only to return more than a thousand years later with a book and a prophet calling for a renewal of the covenant and the old family ties.

THE "TEST" OF ABRAHAM: THE "BINDING" AND NEAR SACRIFICE OF ABRAHAM'S SON

One very interesting place where the Hebrew Bible and the Qur'ān differ in their respective descriptions of Abraham's life is in the matter of the "binding" and near sacrifice of Abraham's son, understood to be Isaac in the Hebrew Bible and Ishmael in most (but not all) Islamic traditions.[2] According to the account recorded in the Hebrew Bible (Gen 22:1–19), sometime after the banishment of Hagar and Ishmael into the wilderness,

> God put Abraham to the test. He said to him, "Abraham," and he answered, "Here I am." And He said, "take your son, your favored one, Isaac, whom you love, and go to the land of Moriah, and offer him there as a burnt offering on one of the heights that I will point out to you." So early next morning, Abraham saddled his ass and took with him two of his servants and his son Isaac.

Three days later, once he had found the appointed place for the sacrifice,

> Abraham took the wood for the burnt offering and put it on his son Isaac. He himself took the firestone and the knife; and the two walked off together. Then Isaac said to his father Abraham, "Father!" And he answered, "Yes, my son." And he said, "Here are the firestone and the wood, but where is the sheep for the burnt offering?" And Abraham said, "God will see to the sheep for His burnt offering, my son." And the two of them walked on together.

2. More will be said of this below.

According to the biblical story, when they reached the appointed place, Abraham built an altar, laid out the wood, bound his son, and laid him on the altar, where he was ready to sacrifice him. Then, at the last minute, an angel called out to him and told him not to raise his hand against the boy. The angel went on to explain that this had been a test, and—now that Abraham's fear of God and devotion were beyond doubt—there was no need to go through with it. Spying a ram caught in a thicket nearby, Abraham proceeded to sacrifice the animal—instead of his son—to God. Then the angel spoke to him again.

> The angel of the Lord called to Abraham a second time from heaven, and said, "By my self, I swear, the Lord declares: Because you have done this and have not withheld your son, your favored one, I will bestow my blessing upon you and make your descendants as numerous as the stars of heaven and the sands on the seashore; and your descendants shall seize the gates of their foes. All the nations of the earth bless themselves by your descendants, because you have obeyed my command. Abraham then returned to his servants, and they departed together for Beer-sheba; and Abraham stayed at Beer-sheba. (Gen 22:1–19)

While this remains the official biblical account, it is interesting to note that alternative versions of this story exist in the oral traditions of Judaism, oral traditions known as the Midrash. In some of these versions, we encounter an Isaac who is fully aware of what is happening, an Isaac who knowingly and willingly offers himself as a sacrifice to God. In this, the Hebrew tradition anticipates or foreshadows the Qur'ānic version of the story:

> Verily, among those who followed in his [Noah's] way was Abraham.
>
> Since he came to his Lord with a sound and wholesome heart
> . . .
>
> [He prayed], "O my Lord! Grant me [a son] from among the righteous!"

So We gave him the good news of a forbearing youth.

Then, when he reached [the age of] walking with him [i.e., his father],

He [Abraham] said, "Oh my son! Verily I see in my dream that I will sacrifice you; so look [and tell me] what you [yourself] can see."

He said, "O my father! Do what you have been commanded, and you will find me—God willing—among those who are patient."

So, when they had both surrendered to God, and [Abraham] had laid him on his forehead,

We called out to him, "O Abraham!

You have already realized your vision!" In this way do We reward the righteous.

Verily this was a clear trial,

and We ransomed him with a great sacrifice.

And We left [this blessing] for him among those who came after,

"Peace be upon Abraham!"

Thus do We reward the righteous,

For, verily, he is among our believing servants.

And we gave him glad tidings of Isaac, a prophet from among the righteous.

And We blessed him and Isaac, but of their progeny there are [both] the righteous and those who do wrong to their own souls. (from the *sūra* of "the Ranks" / *al-ṣaffāt* [37]:83–84, 100–113)

While the Qur'ān does not mention Ishmael by name in its account of the sacrifice, it seems to suggest that the good news of Isaac came to Sarah and Abraham after the event, and so Muslim interpreters have consistently seen Ishmael as the "forbearing youth" who was willing to give up his life in order that Abraham's vision might come to pass.

Even with the differences in chronology and the son selected for sacrifice, however, it is crucial here to note that, in both accounts, the focus is not so much upon which son is going to be sacrificed or when, but rather on the fact that Abraham is willing to "surrender" himself to God's command and offer up that which was most beloved in his eyes. On this, the biblical and Qur'ānic accounts speak with one voice.[3]

~

Bringing our attention back to pre-Islamic Arabia and the origins of Islam, then, we can begin to see how the Arabs understood themselves to be the descendants of Abraham (via Ishmael) and why, when a prophet eventually came to them with "an Arabic recitation," the message was understood to be Abrahamic through and through.

3. Recent years have witnessed a rise of studies that have expanded and deepened our appreciation for the shared legacy (or parallel legacies) of Abraham within the Abrahamic family of religions. See, for example, Bruce Feiler's *Abraham*, Jon D. Levenson's "Abraham Among Jews, Christians, and Muslims" and "Conversion of Abraham to Judaism, Christianity, and Islam." Last but not least are several important works on the topic by Reuven Firestone, incl. *Journeys in Holy Lands*; "Abraham's Association with the Meccan Sanctuary," 365–93; and "Patriarchy, Primogeniture and Polemic."

6

The "Age of Ignorance" and the Dawning of Islam

THE HISTORIES that have come down to us concerning the culture and history of pre-Islamic Arabia were written almost entirely by Muslims long after the establishment of Islam as the dominant religion in Arabia and well after the first generations of Muslims had established an Islamic political/administrative system that dominated a vast portion of the civilized world, from Spain in the west to India in the east. Their views of history were very much a product of their time and experience, just as ours today can be seen as such. Thus, when looking at the polytheistic and tribal world of Arabia prior to the establishment of the "civilizing" force of Islam, they did so with an understandable chip on their shoulders. The "Age of Ignorance" (al-jāhilīya) came to be their preferred way of referring to the worldview, culture, and behavior of the Arabs prior to the dawn of Islam, a dawning that began a new era, marked by the establishment of a new understanding of community and a new way of life under the leadership of the prophet Muhammad and, after him, of his closest companions and family.

To be sure, there are many aspects of the pre-Islamic culture that would strike the modern reader as primitive, perhaps even barbaric. Although some lived in towns and cities, most of the Arabs of the desert were nomadic, which means that they wandered their respective, tribally-established regions of the desert with their camels and flocks of goats and sheep. Living in tents made of animal hides and woven wool carpets and tapestries, they subsisted on a simple diet of meat, milk and milk products (cheeses and yogurts), bread and rice. It was a harsh but highly esteemed way of life, and the pre-Islamic Arabs were a toughened and very proud people. War and intertribal fighting was commonplace and widespread. Some have even referred to this chronic cultural condition of conflict and vendetta as the national sport of the Arabs prior to the coming of Islam (sixth to early seventh century CE).

Some historians now think that at least some of the tribal culture of the ancient Arabs was matriarchal (i.e., dominated by women, in many respects).[1] Polyandry (the practice of a woman marrying more than one man at the same time) seems to have been common; women were known to have remained with their tribe after they married, and their children remained with them, even when the man (or men) to whom she was bound may have come and gone with no permanent presence in her life or the life of her tribe. In the centuries just before the coming of Islam, however, the trends seem to have shifted in the opposite direction. Men dominated the scene, for the most part, and women were kept under the watchful eye of the tribe. Honor and reputation meant everything, and, with the ever-present danger of a tribe being attacked and "shamed" by its women being captured or violated, women were jealously guarded. According to the Qur'ān, which is quite critical of the tribal lifestyle of this period, the jealous guarding of females even went to the extreme of killing infant girls so that the family would not be vulnerable to this kind of shaming. This practice of female infanticide is harshly condemned in the Qur'ān and was not tolerated after the prophet Muhammad had established himself as the main powerbroker of Western Arabia.

In addition to the nomadism and tribalism, the fighting and the infanticide, the Arabs were great lovers of wine, and we have

1. See Leila Ahmed, *Women and Gender in Islam*, 151 and following.

plenty of archeological and literary evidence to indicate that they imported a fair amount of it. Thus, we can easily see much in their life and worldview that served as an easy target for the "civilized" Muslim historians of a later age. One striking exception to this was the fact that, universally throughout the desert, the Arabs were a people that shared a love for poetry.

POETRY

I have spent many late nights awake, listening to teary-eyed old men recite poetry back and forth to one another in Arabic, Persian, Urdu, and other languages we associate with Islamic cultures. In the Arabic speaking world, a poet can draw larger audiences than rock stars or movie stars. In many politically sensitive countries, politically outspoken poets are watched carefully and are often prohibited from public readings. When a famous poet is allowed to recite to a packed stadium or theater, there often is no extravagant stage display: just a poet and a microphone. All this is reflective of a core cultural fact in many Islamic societies: language wields power. This cultural fact reaches back to the pre-Islamic period, when poets were believed to be in connection with supernatural beings. And it should come as no surprise, then, that the core "miracle" and proof of Muhammad's claim to prophecy was linguistic, a "recitation" in Arabic that surpassed all other linguistic forms.

There are many things we still do not know about the situation in Western Arabia before the emergence of the prophet Muhammad and the Islamic movement. There are some things we do know, however, and much of this information—relating to their culture, daily lives, and worldviews—comes to us from the poetry of the time.[2] As odd as it may strike the twenty-first-century reader, the pre-Islamic Arabs—with all their barbarism and uncouth

2. One brief, readable and informative source for pre-Islamic poetry and poetic culture is the chapter on "Pagan Poets" in *Night and Horses and the Desert*, 1–29.

attitudes and behaviors—were universally passionate about their language and poetry. In fact, this was their main, if not sole, artistic form, and their passion for it led to a highly complex linguistic system, which was largely unwritten and yet enjoyed a rich vocabulary and highly evolved grammatical structure. The poems from this period that have been preserved are impressively long and involved, showing incredible linguistic sophistication and rhetorical mastery. More than decorative art, this poetry and the unusual individuals who commanded it wielded tremendous power and influence in pre-Islamic society, both urban and nomadic. In fact, often the words of the most famous poets were more feared than any other weapon known to the pre-Islamic Arabs.

In those days, writes R. A. Nicholson in his 1907 work, *A Literary History of the Arabs,*

> Poetry was no luxury for the cultured few, but the sole medium of literary expression. Every tribe had its poets, who freely uttered what they felt and thought. Their unwritten words "flew across the desert faster than arrows," and came home to the hearts and bosoms of all who heard them. Thus in the midst of outward strife and disintegration a unifying principle was at work. Poetry gave life and currency to an ideal of Arabian virtue (*muruwwa*), which, though based on tribal community of blood and insisting that only ties of blood were sacred, nevertheless became an invisible bond between diverse clans, and formed, whether consciously or not, the basis of a national community of sentiment.[3]

In one of the celebrated poems referred to as the "Hanging Poems"[4] of pre-Islamic Arabia, we encounter the poet Tarafa assailed by grief as he pauses over the abandoned encampment of his beloved's tribe, who left traces in the earth that the poet likens to "tattoo marks on the back of a hand." His companions witness his rather undignified emotional collapse and tell him to shrug it

---

3. Quoted from page 72 of the first paperback edition, 1969; originally published by T. Fisher Unwin in 1907.

4. To be explained below.

off and be brave; meanwhile, he loses them in his recollections of his beloved . . .

> A young gazelle there is in the tribe, dark-lipped, fruit-shaking,
>
> flaunting a double necklace of pearls and topazes,
>
> holding aloof, with the herd grazing in the lush thicket,
>
> nibbling the tips of the arak-fruit, wrapped in her cloak.
>
> Her dark lips part in a smile, teeth like a camomile
>
> on a moist hillock shining amid the virgin sands,
>
> whitened as it were by the sun's rays, all but her gums
>
> that are smeared with collyrium—she gnaws not against them;
>
> a face as though the sun had loosed his mantle upon it,
>
> pure of hue, with not a wrinkle to mar it.

Much like a young man in his first car, he races off to escape his pain: "Ah, but when grief assails me, straightway I ride it off mounted on my swift, lean-flanked camel, night and day racing." Then, after celebrating his own qualities, which include his intemperate love of wine, his squandering of his wealth, and his success with women, he turns to his critics, who—according to him—criticize him on account of his wild and violent life. To them he asks, "Can you keep me alive forever? If you can't avert from me the fate that surely awaits me then pray leave me to hasten it on with what money I've got . . .

> But for three things, that are the joy of a young fellow,
>
> I assure you I wouldn't care when my deathbed visitors arrive—
>
> first, to forestall my critics with a good swig
>
> of crimson wine that foams when the water is mingled in;
>
> second, to wheel at the call of the beleaguered a curve-shanked steed
>
> streaking like the wolf of the thicket you've startled lapping the water;
>
> and third, to curtail the day of showers, such an admirable season,
>
> dallying with a ripe wench under the pole-propped tent,
>
> her anklets and her bracelets seemingly hung on the boughs

of a pliant, unriven gum-tree or castor-shrub.

So permit me to drench my head while there's still life in it,

for I tremble at the thought of the scant draught I'll get when I'm dead.

I'm a generous fellow, one that soaks himself in this lifetime;

you'll know to-morrow, when we're dead, which of us is the thirsty one.[5]

In Arabic, the poet was known as the *shāʿir*, literally, "the one who senses" what remains unknown or unseen to others around him. It should not surprise us, then, that the poets were believed to be in league with the supernatural world, specifically with the *jinn*, the unseen spirits of fire who were and are still believed to inhabit the invisible world that engulfs the visible world of humankind. This ancient idea of a human-*jinn* connection is where the modern Arabic word for "insane" (*majnūn*) originates, for it means literally "possessed by the *jinn*." In any case, supernatural possession and/or inspiration was the only way common people could account for the uncanny powers of the poets, who were able to compose lengthy and complex verse of precise meter and rhyme extemporaneously, right on the spot. There was no waste bin full of crumpled papers beside the desk of the composer; on the contrary, the poet—often unable to read or write—was seen to compose on his feet, letting the verse loose in perfect and final form the first time. The poet would then recite his new composition (or, better said, oration) to a circle of "reciters," and they would memorize it to his satisfaction before going forth as living keepers of the poet's compositions. This was the way the poets "published" and became known beyond their tribe throughout the desert.[6]

5. These excerpts come from the ode of Tarafah, one of the most celebrated pre-Islamic poets. The translation is that of A. J. Arberry, *Seven Odes*, 83–89.

6. For a concise and reliable summary of pre-Islamic life and culture, see Frederick Denny's chapter on "Pre-Islamic Arabia" in *Introduction to Islam*, 29–43.

The folk history of the Arabs tells of an annual meeting or poetry festival that was held outside of Mecca, a gathering where the most prominent poets of the day would come together and recite their best compositions. Each year, they say, the festival winner would have the honor of seeing his poem written in gold letters on a large tapestry, which was draped over the cubical structure of the Ka'ba, and there it would hang until the next year's competition. This is the story behind the poems known as the "Hanging Poems" (*al-mu'allaqāt*), and whether it is true or not is perhaps less important than the fact that these "Hanging Poems" were indeed remembered in the subsequent Islamic period and are still treasured today as examples of the tremendous linguistic achievement of the "Age of Ignorance."

RELIGION AND COMMERCE

Turning to the topic of religion in the pre-Islamic period, there is little question that the vast majority of the pre-Islamic Arabs were polytheistic, worshiping an array of gods, goddesses, and spirits. Also well established is the fact that Mecca was celebrated as at least a regional shrine town, a hub for cultic pilgrimage and ritual. Among the Arabs who lived in the region there seems to have been somewhat universal agreement that Abraham and Ishmael were responsible for building the central shrine of Mecca, but this did not keep them from housing hundreds of tribal gods and goddesses in the Ka'ba. Favorite among these gods and goddesses were three known as the "daughters of Allāh"—al-Lāt, al-'Uzza, and al-Manāt.

Scattered across the desert, living in the midst of the polytheistic Arab tribes were Jewish communities, and some of them had attained a degree of prominence and power in Western Arabia. The Jewish tribes of Yathrib (later Medina) and Khaybar were among these. Some Arab tribes, such as that of Ghassān in the northwest (along the Byzantine frontier) had converted to Christianity, and there is some evidence to suggest the presence of Christian ascetic hermits living in various places throughout the desert. In other words, while it might be a stretch to call Arabia a haven of religious and ethnic diversity, the religious and ethnic make up of the western desert knew some complexity.

Adding still another element to this picture, the Qur'ān makes use of a term that may suggest another religious current running through the desert. Referring to Abraham as neither a Jew nor a Christian, the Qur'ān labels him as a "righteous monotheist" or *ḥanīf* (see, for example, *āl ʿimrān* [3]:67, 95),[7] who was associated with *milla*, a particular practice or confession (see *al-baqara* [2]:130, 135; *āl ʿimrān* [3]:95; *al-nisāʾ* [4]:125; *al-anʿām* [6]:161). While an exact rendering of these terms is hard to achieve, the Qur'ānic intention of the first is clearly tied to issues of sincerity (see *al-anʿām* [6]:79), devotion, total surrendering of self, keeping an unwavering commitment to monotheism (see *āl ʿimrān* [3]:67, 95), and living in an ethical manner. The second term (*milla*) is more difficult to pin down, for it seems to suggest a confession and a practice, although we have little to no information about such a "religion" in Arabia prior to the dawn of Islam. Some scholars, such as F. E. Peters, have convincingly suggested that there existed a monotheistic tradition associated with Abraham and Kaʿba in western Arabia,[8] and so there may have been an indigenous monotheistic tradition in the desert that included some basic beliefs and practices associated with Abraham. Given this possibility, it is quite feasible that the young Muhammad came to be associated with members of this Abrahamic "tradition" while growing up in Mecca.

We know that, prior to the time of Muhammad, Mecca's privileged status as a shrine town opened a door to commercial activity and prosperity. While some scholarly disagreement over the scale of this commercial boom continues, nearly all historians

7. For more Qur'ānic references to the Abrahamic "Hanifiyya" tradition, see Peters, *Reader on Classical Islam*, 40–42.

8. See his *Muhammad and the Origins of Islam*, 122–30.

agree that, because of the annual pilgrimage to the Ka'ba, the leading entrepreneurs of Mecca were able to negotiate safe passage for their caravans to Yemen in the south all the way up to Byzantium and Sassanian Persia to the north. This gave the Meccans additional access to ancient, refined civilizations and their respective religions. It also gave them an incentive to maintain the polytheistic status quo of the town, for the annual months of polytheistic pilgrimage afforded them regular opportunities for renewing their tribal contacts and negotiations. To wipe away the polytheistic pilgrimage was to wipe away the very foundation of Mecca's prosperity, however modest or opulent it might have been.

We can thus see that an interesting stage was set for a modestly successful, middle-aged Meccan to stand up in the city center and preach a predictably unpopular message: forsaking the worship of all gods save one: "Allāh"—literally, THE God, the high god of the Meccan pantheon and the "father" of the popular goddesses known as the "daughters of Allāh." More, the message made extravagant claims of authority for the messenger and claimed knowledge of the afterlife as well as the unseen world of the *jinn* and the angels. As proof of his prophetic authority, this man brought forth a poetic, linguistic recitation that claimed to have been "sent down" from God through the mediation of the angel Gabriel. Describing itself as the definitive restatement of earlier scriptures and the renewal of the religion of Abraham (*millat Ibrāhīm*), this enigmatic recitation challenged the very foundation of the Meccans' worldview and way of life, and many did not appreciate the challenge.

Such is the story that begins the epic history of the uncompromisingly monotheistic, Abrahamic movement we call Islam.

7

Prophecy

Muhammad and the Advent of Qur'ānic Revelations in Mecca

*I*WAS *holding on to my seat as the Land Rover whipped around blind mountain corners at hair-raising speeds. Returning from a shrine visit high in the mountains above Islamabad, we were trying to get back to the city before dark. Around almost every turn in the road we encountered traffic—trucks, cars, donkeys pulling carts, pedestrians—all seemingly unconcerned by the life-threatening activity whizzing by them in every direction. The Sufi shaykh, who insisted on taking the wheel that late afternoon, laughed about driving with nūr al-baṣīrah (the light of mystical vision or insight) as he sped down the mountain roads and sang along with the hymns of love for the Prophet playing on the car stereo. Gradually, I was forced to let go and fall under the sway of the breathtakingly beautiful songs as the sun began to sink and the cool air of the mountains gave way to the warmer breezes of the lowlands.*

Almost two decades prior to this experience in northern Pakistan, I had the privilege of taking graduate level courses within the College of Islamic Studies at the University of Jordan. Although I was impressed with all of my teachers there, my Qur'ānic Sciences teacher was something of a local legend—a blind scholar with a critical mind, oceanic knowledge, and penetrating insight. Even after so many years, I recall him vividly: a sweet yet demanding and commanding man who could seemingly see through us—his graduate students—whenever we gathered for class, be it in the official classroom at the University of Jordan's College of Sharīʿah or in his living room. Having just arrived from Toronto with my comprehensive exams for the PhD behind me and being the only one in the class not already familiar with him, I could sense that my fellow graduate students both loved and feared him. I suppose I enjoyed a slightly more casual relationship with him due to the fact that I was coming from a western educational model in which faculty and graduate students routinely enjoy more informal and dialectical relationships, but I could tell that the love-fear reverence for him and for his learning steadily grew within me the more I was in his presence.

It seemed to us that he had memorized every book in the library. Nothing escaped him; even if we had questions formulating in the deep recesses of our minds, it seemed that he could sense them, for he would break through the silence with "yaa shaykh Timothy! Esh suʾaalak? Isʾal!" ("Shaykh Timothy! What is your question? Ask it!") There was no hiding from his spiritual gaze.

One time, when we were having class at home in his living room, we (males and females) sat in a large circle tracing the periphery of the room. The walls behind us were loaded with beautifully bound Arabic works of exegesis, theology, history, philosophy, etc. Apparently, like me, he had gone to graduate school with an interest in Islamic philosophy, but his teachers prevailed upon him to do his doctorate in the Qurʾānic sciences. In any case, on that occasion, we were discussing a point in the famous classical exegesis of al-Ṭabarī. He called out to "shaykh Ziyad," one of the students, to reach above him and pull out the third volume of the multi-volume work. Startled, Ziyad looked above him and—sure enough—found the text right above his head. Then, our professor instructed him to turn to a specific page some one or two hundred pages into the volume and to begin reading. Ziyad opened the book, found the first full paragraph on the specified page, and began reading. "No!" our dear professor called out, "Next paragraph!" Such was his scholarly erudition.

The memory that wins for him a place in this chapter comes from a class when we were discussing the historical situations in the Prophet's life that "occasioned" the sending down of certain Qur'ānic revelations. As he was describing the indignities and insults suffered by the Prophet while he still resided among his relatives in his hometown of Mecca, this great scholar began to weep in class. We were spell-bound, silent, afraid to say anything, afraid to interrupt this moment of unexpected vulnerability, and so we all cast our eyes down and waited for his sobbing to subside. Such was his love for the Prophet.

The love of the prophet Muhammad is a tangible force that pervades all aspects of Islamic piety in virtually all denominations of Islamic theology and law. In addition to the many ways Muslims try to emulate the Prophet's noble manners, dress, and religious practice, they frequently remember him in speeches, poems (often called "*qaṣīdah*" poems or "odes"), devotional gatherings, and in popular devotional hymns (called "*nashīd*" hymns), composed in every imaginable language, including English of course. Such hymns are traditionally sung *a capella*, or without instrumental accompaniment, with the exception of an occasional hand drum. That said, there is a rapidly growing number of Muslim *nashīd* artists who use instrumental accompaniment in their devotional hymns and love songs for the Prophet. In order to give just a "taste" of such expressions of devotion, all one has to do is conduct a web search of the words "nashid" and "prophet" or visit websites such as www.thenasheedshop.com or search the online recordings and music videos of internationally-known *nashīd* composers and singers, artists such as Sami Yusuf, a British Muslim singer-songwriter, composer, producer and musician,[1] who stands among the more contemporary variety of *nashīd* artists who use instrumental music to accompany their devotional hymns. While there are literally too many established and up-and-coming *nashīd* composers and performers to mention here, even those who sing predominantly in English, some other English-language *nashīd* artists include Canadian singer-songwriter-poet Dawud Wharnsby, South African singer-songwriter Zain Bhikha, Australian imam-translator-singer-community activist Belal Asaad, and, of course, the UK's Yusuf Islam (Cat Stevens).

One of Sami Yusuf's famous early songs extolling the virtues of the Prophet is entitled, "*al-Mu'allim*" or "the Teacher," and serves as a moving example of this style of Muslim piety. The song celebrates the prophet Muhammad's mercy, compassion, universal benevolence and concern, self-sacrifice, and world-transforming legacy. While unique to this Muslim artist, songs such as this are beyond number and in every language known to Muslims. They serve as both a token of the community's love for the Prophet and a tool for softening hearts and cultivating an ever-deepening appreciation and love for his person. In the light of this love and appreciation, the Prophet transcends his place in history and becomes an eternal archetype for living the godly life.

Although the prophet Muhammad lived much closer to our time than Jesus, Buddha, Moses, and other towering religious figures and prophets from the distant past, scholars admit that we still have much to learn about the life of the Prophet. His life example (*sunnah*) was remembered by his companions and passed down to subsequent generations via oral transmission, but his narrative biography (*sīrah*) and the nonnarrative record of his words and

---

1. Complete lyrics to this and other songs can be found at www.samiyusuf .com.

deeds (*ḥadīth* collections) were put into writing more than a century after his death (in 632 of the "Common Era" or CE). Thus, from the very beginning of this written history, scholars have had reason to question the reliability of each part of the story and each deed or statement situated within the story. While many aspects of the Prophet's biography have since been painstakingly verified and "tested" in the light of the Qur'ānic record and the well-known and documented parts of the story, parts of the historical record continue to be questioned by scholars both within and without the ranks of the believers. Acknowledging this ongoing scholarly quest for "the historical Muhammad," I will try to lay before you the narrative that the majority of scholars, both Muslim and non-Muslim, uphold as the standard biography.[2]

The precise year of the Prophet's birth is not known for certain. Traditional biographies date his birth to the year during which an Ethiopian Christian force invaded the Yemen (in South Arabia) and began pushing northward toward Mecca. As their fighting force is believed to have included elephants, the year was remembered in Arabia as the "Year of the Elephant." Historians have verified this invasion, apparently precipitated by the alleged persecution of Christians under a Jewish king in the Yemen, and they have determined the year 570 as the year in which this event probably occurred. If the Muslim biographers of the Prophet are correct, then, Muhammad was born in or around the year 570 CE, roughly five and a half centuries after the time of Jesus' active ministry and passion in Jerusalem.

2. There are a number of standard and responsible biographies written by both Muslim scholars and scholars of other faiths; these include the classic works of W. M. Watt (*Muhammad at Mecca*, *Muhammad at Medina*, and *Muhammad Prophet and Statesman*), a biography by the late Martin Lings (*Muhammad*), the more recent scholarly work of F. E. Peters (*Muhammad and the Origins of Islam*), and others. My synopsis of the Prophet's biography here is intentionally intuitive and synthetic, drawing upon all of these and other sources as I try to display the Prophet's life in a manner that is simple, clear, fair-minded, and yet also reflective of traditional Muslim understandings.

From the biographical record and our understanding of pre-Islamic culture, it seems that Muhammad's early life was a mildly troubled one, for his father died while he was still in his mother's womb. By Arabian standards, this meant that he was born an orphan to his mother Āminah, who began to raise him in his paternal grandfather's home in Mecca. This orphan status would have been a "stain" or stigmatizing factor in any Meccan boy's life, and we have no reason to believe that the boy Muhammad was any different. After a few years, both his grandfather and mother died, and so the growing boy was passed to his father's brother, the man known in history as "Abū Ṭālib," for care and custody. Thus, Muhammad effectively grew up and attained maturity in his uncle's home, where we can assume he was exposed to the prevailing culture and livelihood of Mecca.

It is worthy of note here that Abū Ṭālib, indeed like Muhammad himself, was a member of the Quraysh tribe, the elite but rather large inter-related group of families that made up Mecca's business and cultural elite. Abū Ṭālib's family was not the leading family within the tribe by far, but their privileged place within the Quraysh tribe and the larger societal scene cannot be ignored. Indeed, Abū Ṭālib's prestige within the larger family is perhaps best evidenced by the fact that, following Muhammad's claim to prophecy (well into his adult years) and its subsequent rejection by the leaders of the Quraysh, Abū Ṭālib's personal prestige and patronage of Muhammad prevented anyone—Qurayshi or not—from physically attacking Muhammad. The "Law of Retaliation" (*lex talionis*)—perhaps the only universal law upheld within pre-Islamic Arabia—meant that any attack on Muhammad would have been taken as an attack upon Abū Ṭālib and his family, and no one seems to have felt up to the challenge.

Returning to Muhammad's early life, then, we can say with some confidence that Muhammad began a career in regional trade. According to the traditional biography, the young Muhammad earned a reputation for righteousness in his dealings, and this caught the attention of a moderately wealthy widow, Khadījah, who offered the now adult Muhammad the opportunity of managing her business affairs. His acceptance of this offer and his admirable performance in this new position inspired her to make him another, even greater offer. In this way, he soon became her husband, in spite of the fact that he was her junior by some years.

By all accounts, they enjoyed an excellent marriage, and Muhammad benefited greatly from their union. For one thing, he began to enjoy leisure time; something his previous working life probably did not afford him. This proved to be a crucial development in the pre history of Islam, for Muhammad began using that leisure time to make regular retreats in the rocky wilderness surrounding the trade town of his youth. We are not quite sure what he did during these retreats, but a regimen of prayer, fasting, and almsgiving were certainly a part of his retreat practice, and there seems to be indication that these retreats became increasingly regular following his marriage. Again, according to the earliest biographical accounts, he made a habit of fasting in retreat for one month every year, and, when he completed his month, he would reenter the city of Mecca and walk around the Ka'ba seven or more times before returning to his house.

Although there remains some speculation about the content of the first Qur'ānic revelation or "recitation" given to Muhammad, all Muslims are unified in the belief that it was here, in the rocky wilderness outside of Mecca, that the angel Gabriel first appeared to Muhammad and began dispensing the recitations that would later make up "THE recitation"—the Qur'ān—believed by Muslims to be the final message sent to humanity prior to the final judgment.

The biography explains that Muhammad was sleeping in a cave on or near Mount Ḥirā', when he experienced a decidedly supernatural and most unnerving vision. A being Muhammad later described as "filling the horizon" appeared before him and held up a cloth of brocade upon which there was writing. The being then commanded Muhammad to "read" or "recite" (in Arabic, both are represented by the same command, "*iqra'!*"). Frightened, Muhammad said that he could not read. The cloth tablets were then pressed down upon him so severely that he thought he would suffocate, and then the being let up and again commanded Muhammad to recite. Three times Muhammad explained that he could not read, and three times the tablets were pressed down upon him so that he thought he was going to die. Finally, when the being presented Muhammad with the brocade a fourth time and commanded him to recite, Muhammad wisely changed his response by asking what he was supposed to recite. What followed is widely held to be the very first installment of Qur'ānic revelations:

> Recite! In the name of your Lord, who created,
>
> created the human person from a clinging clot.
>
> Recite! And your Lord is the most Generous,
>
> Who taught by means of the Pen,
>
> taught the human being that which he did not [previously] know. (from *sūra[t] al-'Alaq* / "the clinging clot" [96]:1–5)

Soon after, Muhammad is reported to have gone out onto the mountain, where he beheld a giant winged man who filled his vision every direction he turned, a man who identified himself as the archangel and who announced that Muhammad had been chosen to be the messenger of Allāh. Filled with worries about being possessed or having gone mad, Muhammad is reported to have contemplated ending his own life right then and there, but his close and trusting relationship with Khadījah gave him comfort and led him to seek counsel among people of knowledge in such matters. According to several early accounts, Khadījah took him to see her cousin, an old man named Waraqa ibn Nawfal, who was said to have been a man of great learning and wisdom in matters of religion. In one early tradition, he is said to have been one of four pre-Islamic Meccans who stood apart from the polytheistic rites and condemned the practices of their time; accusing their

contemporaries of upholding a corruption of Abraham's faith and
practice, they went out in search of the true "ḥanīf" way associated
with Abraham. In the course of his search, Waraqa is said to have
learned Hebrew and converted to Christianity.[3] In any case, once
Muhammad explained to Waraqa what he had seen and experienced, Waraqa became the first to recognize him as the recipient of
prophecy: "This is the *nāmus* which God sent down unto Moses."[4]

We have no reason to assume that Muhammad, at this stage,
had much sense of what lay in store, including the social mission
with which he was about to be charged, but, as the Qur'ānic episodes with Gabriel became more frequent and more content-rich,
it was made clear to Muhammad that he was being charged with
a task:

> O you wrapped up [in a cloak]!
>
> Get up and give warning!
>
> Magnify your Lord!
>
> Purify your garments,
>
> and shun all abomination!
>
> Do not [in giving] expect [personal] increase,
>
> Be patient for the sake of your Lord
>
> (from *sūra[t] al-Mudaththir* / "the one wrapped up" [74]:1–7)

In addition to the denial of all gods save the One, Allāh, the
earliest themes of Qur'ānic revelation stressed many of the core
doctrines explained in chapter 3 of this text, doctrines that were
not very attractive or even compelling to the pre-Islamic Arabs:
the surety of the afterlife and judgment; the ethical imperative of
living righteously and caring for the destitute and the weak (esp.
the widow and the orphan); the miracle of the natural world—
now seen as a proof of its Divine authorship; the tradition of the

---

3. For quick reference, see Peters, *Reader on Classical Islam*, 41. For more
detailed information concerning this figure, see Uri Rubin's chapter, "Khadija-
Waraqa Story" in *Eye of the Beholder*, 103–12.

4. Rubin, *Eye of the Beholder*, 107.

prophets of old, among whom Muhammad was now counted as heir, seal, and brother; and God's all-powerful will and providence, a teaching that included Allāh's active involvement in human affairs.

In other words, Muhammad was called to return to his native city of Mecca and proclaim a message that was sure to be unwelcome: to forsake the worship of the many favored deities of the Ka'ba in favor of worshiping only Allāh, the "high" god of the Meccan pantheon. This, in turn, meant that the Quraysh tribe, hitherto a law unto themselves, would be obligated to follow the orphan Muhammad, now proclaimed to be the chosen prophet of Allāh on earth, or else risk being cast forever in the hellfire of an afterlife that they did not believe in anyway. It also meant that the proud tribesmen would have to swallow their pride and become the "slaves" of Allāh, who ordered them to share their wealth with the poor, to change many aspects of their proud and brutal culture, and to prostrate themselves on the earth in worship, fear, and awe of Him. An easy sell? No way.

And so we see how the stage was set for rejection, struggle, exile, and—eventually—a triumphal, heroic return to the city that said no. So begins the historic venture of Islam, a movement that was simultaneously religious and political, spiritual and social, a wave that would, within less than a century of the Prophet's death in 632 CE, sweep across the known world and establish an empire stretching from Spain in the west to the borders of India and China in the east.

8

Archetypes, Prototypes, and the Perfection of Religion

Contemplating Medina as a Prototype for Muslim Societies and a Challenging Articulation of "Real" Islam

I was fourteen years old when footage of the 1979 Islamic revolution in Iran and the United States hostage crisis filled American TV screens. Jimmy Carter was president, but his presence in the overall coverage was minimal in comparison to the Ayatollah Khomeini, who was for Americans the literal face of the revolution in Iran. Other leading activist ayatollahs were seldom mentioned, and the ousted Shah was almost completely out of the picture. Certainly, with American property destroyed and American lives in danger, and later with a death threat against novelist Salman Rushdie in the air, there was no room in the news for the Shah's terrible record on human rights or the real grievances underlying the anti-American anger that fuelled the revolution. Thus, for me and for most Americans, the Ayatollah Khomeini became a symbol of rabid extremism, irrational anti-American fury and vengeance, and a deadly enemy of the American way. This remained my general, unchallenged impression until I began graduate studies in Canada.

In my second or third year of graduate studies, I was serving as a Teaching Assistant for a somewhat large Introduction to Islam

98

*course at the University of Toronto, a course in which every imag-
inable Muslim denomination was well represented, not to mention
students from other faiths and no faith at all. In the course of my
duties, I used to hold regular office hours during which I would help
the students with their coursework and exam preparation. One day,
as I sat with a young Muslim student, I noticed that he had a picture of a smiling, beaming Ayatollah Khomeini glued to the cover
of his notebook. Needless to say, this caught my attention. I asked
him, "Is that who I think it is?" Sitting tall and proud, he replied in
a tone filled with admiration, "Yes. It's Ayatollah Khomeini." Sensing
that his Ayatollah Khomeini was quite different than the Ayatollah
I had been presented, I said, "Please, tell me about him." Thus began
a learning experience that initiated me in the crucial importance of
perspective: how one concrete thing can look dramatically different
when approached through a different lens or from a different angle.
In the end, of course, no one angle or perspective can claim to be
the universally-binding, singular truth, and so my preprogrammed,
media-driven picture of the Ayatollah had to make room for a man
who wrote mystical love poetry and lived very simply, a man who
was deeply loved and spiritually emulated by millions of people, a
man who just may have had a guiding vision that was very different
from the brutal and unseemly aspects of what became known as the
"Islamic Revolution."*

*Whatever our understanding of this twentieth-century figure,
there can be no doubt that he represents a current within Islamic
thought that envisions the political life as a necessary extension of
the religious life, the state as a vehicle for the religious aspirations of
the community. In his own words,*

> Islam is the religion of the strugglers who want right and
> justice, the religion of those demanding freedom and inde-
> pendence and those who do not want to allow the infidels to
> dominate the believers.

> But the enemies have portrayed Islam in a different light. They
> have drawn from the minds of the ordinary people a distorted
> picture of Islam and implanted this picture even in the reli-

gious academies. The enemies' aim behind this was to extinguish the flame of Islam and to cause its vital revolutionary character to be lost, so that the Muslims would not think of seeking to liberate themselves and to implement all the rules of their religion through the creation of a government that guarantees their happiness under the canopy of an honorable human life.

They have said that Islam has no relationship whatsoever with organizing life and society or with creating a government of any kind and that it only concerns itself with the rules of menstruation and childbirth. It may contain some ethics. But beyond this, it has no bearing on issues of life and of organizing society . . .

. . . The Qur'ānic phrases concerned with society's affairs are many times the phrases concerned with private worship. In any of the detailed ḥadīth books, you can hardly find more than three or four chapters concerned with regulating man's private worship and man's relationship with God and few chapters dealing with ethics. The rest is strongly connected with social and economic affairs, with human rights, with administration and with the policy of societies . . .

This is our situation. The enemies have implanted these falsehoods in the minds of people in cooperation with their agents, have ousted Islam's judiciary and political laws from the sphere of application and have replaced them by European laws in contempt of Islam for the purpose of driving it away from society . . . In the Prophet's time, was the church separated from the state? Were there at the time theologians and politicians? At the time of the Caliphs and the time of 'Ali, the Commander of the faithful, was the state separated from the church? Was there an agency for the church and another for the state?

. . . Considering that the implementation forever of laws after the venerable Prophet, may God's prayers be upon him, is one of the essentials of life, then it is necessary for government to exist and for this government to have the qualities of an executive and administrative authority. Without this, social chaos, corruption, and ideological and moral deviation would

prevail. This can be prevented only through the creation of a
just government that runs all aspects of life.[1]

Whether Islam does or does not unequivocally call for the
establishment of a religious state remains an open question that
Muslims continue to debate. On the side opposing Khomeini,
a growing number of Muslim scholars argue that, following the
death of the Prophet in 632 CE, such a state would violate the clear
Qur'ānic injunction forbidding compulsion in matters of religion.
In other words, no Muslim can morally enforce his or her interpretation of Islam upon another through the coercive power of the
state, and so the best solution is a state that is religiously neutral.
This will be touched upon again at the end of the chapter. In any
case, whatever view one espouses, it is a fact that all sides of this
debate take us back to the life of the Prophet, specifically to the
final decade of his life, when his spiritual and religious mission
involved gathering and guiding a community through persecution, armed conflict, and the many challenges—domestic and
external—of a nascent nation.

THE HIJRAH / MIGRATION OF 622 CE

As we have mentioned earlier in this book, anyone who has fled
from a dangerous or threatening situation to a place of safety has
made *hijrah*. Anyone who has courageously said "no more" or "not
today" to a destructive, unhealthy habit or relationship or situation
and begun a journey to something better has made *hijrah*. Anyone
who has broken free from a cage of restriction and entrapment,
where all possibilities are closed and the light of hope has been
all but blocked, and set out in search of a new place of hope and
possibility and freedom has made *hijrah*. *Hijrah* is the dynamic
principle that animates the very foundations of lived Islam, for it
represents the daily migration to a better place, a better state, leading ultimately to a blessed reunion with the One who made us and

1. Donohue and Esposito, *Islam in Transition*, 332–35.

opened up the prophetic pathways for us to come home. *Hijrah* also stands unshakably as the cornerstone of Islam in history, for it was only after the Prophet made his historic migration to Medina (then "Yathrib") that Islam, as a complete religion and way of life, came into full realization. For this reason, Muslims have ever regarded the year of his *hijrah* as the first year of the Islamic calendar.

As we have seen above, unable to transform Meccan society from within, Muhammad found himself forced out by an increasingly threatening and hostile opposition. Having sent his companions and their families ahead, little by little, to join the converts in Yathrib for months, he and his friend, Abū Bakr, stole away in the night with ʿAlī remaining behind to serve as a decoy for the Prophet's enemies. Escaping the pursuit of his now hostile relatives and other Meccan enemies, he and Abū Bakr eventually arrived in the oasis town and so began what was to be the most formative period of Muhammad's prophetic career. Now, for the very first time, the community was free to assemble and establish the complete and comprehensive way of life described in chapter 4. Now, for the very first time, the Prophet was able to lay foundations for a more organized and systematic expression of monotheism, foundations that—for many—are believed to manifest the ultimate synthesis of politics and religion in Islam.

THE PACT OF MEDINA

While we cannot go as far as to say that Muhammad established a "state" in the modern sense of the word, we can affirm that he took steps that may be called political. One of the first such steps he reportedly took was essentially an attempt to establish a contractual bond between all of the tribes and individuals of Yathrib, a bond that was intended to seal the fate of the Muslims—both those of Meccan origin and those native to Yathrib—to the fates of the Jewish tribes and other groups present in Yathrib at that time. This attempt is often called the "constitution" or "pact" of Medina, and it basically served as a written inventory of the major tribes and groups present in Yathrib at that time. More,

> The pact attempted to put an end to all intertribal feuding and vendetta within Yathrib society, which had been deeply troubled by intertribal violence and vendetta prior to the prophet Muhammad's coming.

> In place of the "law of retaliation," the pact sought to lay the groundwork for individual (non collective) prosecution and for nonviolent dispute resolution, with financial compensation for loss of property and life and with God and the Prophet being the final arbitrators in cases that cannot be resolved in any other way.

> Far from insisting that everyone in Yathrib convert to Islam, the pact promised religious freedom and tolerance for the Jews and for the other groups present in the city and even went so far as to guarantee equal religious rights for all.

> Clearly aware of the possibility that the Prophet's Meccan enemies might try to meddle in Medinan politics and threaten the Muslims from a distance, the pact pledged mutual protection and fidelity to one another ("the people of the document") above all other allegiances and made it a crime to associate with enemies without the express permission of Muhammad.

> Clearly stating that each group must pay its own way in times of war, the agreement sought to ensure financial fairness in the event that the city was attacked or went to war.

In sum, then, the pact can be seen as a contractual attempt to establish a multi-tribal and multi-faith federation within Yathrib; and, because it was crafted at the Prophet's behest and under his careful scrutiny, it can also be seen as the prototype for all future

Islamic societies and systems of government.[2] Many have indeed taken it as such.

It is important to note here that Muhammad did not wield the power of a monarch or universally accepted messenger of God in this federation; rather, he seems to have played the role of a facilitator and universally trusted arbitrator. There were, no doubt, some in Yathrib who were not eager to be importing Muhammad's problems, especially his hostile relations with the powerful Meccan Quraysh, but Yathrib had its own serious problems, and Muhammad offered a way out of the immediate mess. Everyone thus seems to have signed on, an act that made them part of the "people of the document" and bound them to Muhammad and the Muslims. As we will see below, these new bonds had profound implications.

THE ADVENT OF QUR'ĀNICALLY-SANCTIONED VIOLENCE AND THE ENSUING STORY OF CONFLICT, NEGOTIATION, FORGIVENESS, AND TRANSFORMATION

With the Prophet now safely in Medina and the community (*ummah*) putting down roots, the Qur'ān makes many significant moves, including long and detailed revelations that seek to regulate and optimize community life. One of the most significant and far-reaching of these socially-or politically-oriented moves was the granting of permission to the Muslim refugees from Mecca to take up arms against the Meccan polytheists who had driven them out.

In other words, while the Muslims had never engaged in hostilities with their Meccan antagonists while in Mecca, the Qur'ān now opens the doors to religiously justified armed conflict. It is important here to note that there is no Qur'ānic phrase or teaching that can be accurately rendered as "holy war"; indeed, the

2. Many complete translations of the agreement can now be found online, but one might begin with a reliable and time-tested, scholarly rendering in Watt's *Muhammad at Medina*.

admission of violence seems to be a Qur'ānic acknowledgment of humanity's corruption, stubborn opposition to clear "Divine signs" given to them, and violent persecution of the prophets. This can be seen in what most scholars consider to be the first of these "war verses," dated very early in the Medinan period, sometime after the pact of Medina was drafted and signed.

> To those against whom war is made, permission is given [to fight], because they are wronged; Verily, God is utterly powerful in helping them; [Such are] those who have been expelled unjustly from their homes, [for no reason] other than that they say, "Our Lord is God." Had God not repelled some people by means of others, monasteries, churches, synagogues, and mosques, [places] in which the name of Allāh is abundantly commemorated, would surely have been destroyed. Allāh will certainly aid those who aid His cause. Verily God is [infinitely] Strong, ever Mighty.
>
> [Those to whom permission is here given and who aid God's cause] are those who, if We establish them in the land, establish regular prayer and give regular charity, enjoin the right and forbid wrong; and the end of (all) affairs resides with God.
>
> If they seek to misrepresent you as false, [know that] so did the peoples before them—the People of Noah, and 'Ād and Thamud; Those of Abraham and Lot; And the folk of Madyan; and Moses was [also] rejected [by Pharaoh and also by his own people]. But I gave some slack to the ungrateful rejecters, after which I took hold of them. How [great] was the disavowal [of them]!
>
> How many sinful towns have We destroyed . . . Do they not journey through the land, so that they might have hearts with which they contemplate or ears by which they might listen? Alas it is not the eyes that are blind, but the hearts in the breasts . . . (*sūra[t] al-ḥajj* [22]:39–46)

While there are many nuances worthy of note in this passage, we will focus only upon a few basic points. First, the Qur'ān clearly indicates that, in the case of the Muslim emigrants now living in Medina, the permission to fight is granted because their antagonists had already committed acts of war against them: expelling them from their homes for no reason other than that they had declared monotheism (see our discussion of the *shahādah* or first "pillar" in chapter 4). What is here presented, then, is a theological formulation of just war rather than a glorification of violence for its own sake. Indeed, the Qur'ān continues to assert that such defensive fighting was permitted in the earlier revelations as a way of protecting the prophetic communities as well as Jewish synagogues, Christian churches and monasteries, Muslim mosques, and other houses of monotheistic worship.

Another point worth noting here is that the Qur'ān offers a vision of the ultimate goal to which fighting should lead: i.e., a society where the laws are just and where people are allowed to worship and live according to their faith. In other words, the Qur'ānic argument is that sometimes violent struggle is required for the establishment of a society that stands for justice and religious freedom. Some familiar with Latin American Catholic theology of the mid twentieth century might thus see this as a Qur'ānic blend of just war theory with a non-Christocentric articulation of "Liberation Theology"—a theological argument for social, economic, and political justice.

> And how can you not fight in God's way while there are weak and vulnerable men and women and children who say, "O our Lord! Deliver us from this town of oppressors and, from Your grace, bring forth for us someone who will keep us safe . . ."
> (4:75–76)

Even in the subsequent "war verses," which tend to get progressively aggressive against the belligerent enemies of the Muslims, now based in Medina, we find that war is never glorified or seen as an end in itself; rather, fighting is seriously regulated and framed as a step toward a more just, more godly society, wherein the rule of law makes fighting no longer necessary. Any characterization of the war verses that does not keep them within their overall context of creating a just society is politically reckless and academically irresponsible, for—if one truly attends to the Qur'ānic context of these verses (both within the Qur'ān and within the history of the Prophet's life)—one finds that the vision of a just and godly society is ever-present.

Indeed, this wider "context" places war within a wider frame of forgiveness, reconciliation, and transformation.[3] One of the most beautiful and moving accounts of forgiveness in the Qur'ān is also a biblical account. Called "the most beautiful of stories," the story of Yūsuf (Joseph) and his brothers stands apart from all other Qur'ānic chapters in that it is the only sustained narrative in the text; indeed, the entire *sūra* is devoted to this one story. In essence, it is a heroic story of envy, violence, injustice, longsuffering, patience, and ultimate exaltation that climaxes with a finale of Divine and human forgiveness. Joseph's brothers—the very same who had thrown him into a well, sold him into slavery, and lied about the entire episode to their father, Jacob—stand before his throne in Egypt. They do not recognize him until he reveals his identity.

> They said, are you indeed Joseph?" He said, "I am Joseph, and this is my brother [Benjamin]. God has indeed been gracious to us! Behold, whosoever is God-conscious and patient, God will never suffer the reward of the righteous to be lost.
>
> They said, "By God! God has indeed preferred you over us. Certainly we were sinners!"
>
> [Then] he said, "Today there is no blame on you. God will forgive [everything] for you. He is the Most Merciful of all those who show mercy.

---

3. The majority of what follows in this chapter is based upon one section of a paper I wrote on Muslim leadership for the Fourth Meeting of the Elijah Board of World Religious Leaders (Haifa and the Galilee, October, 2009). The theme of the meeting was "The Future of Religious Leadership," and so this paper was one of several, each crafted by a scholar practitioner of his/her faith tradition. A web-formatted version of my paper can be found on my blog at www.islamicilluminations.blogspot.com, and the full list of papers can be found at www.elijah-interfaith.org/programs/board-of-world-religious -leaders/fourth-meeting-of-the-bwrl.html.

Liberated by Joseph's clemency and the promise of God's forgiveness, they go back to their father, Jacob, whose sight has been restored by the casting of Joseph's shirt over his face.

> They said, "O our father! Ask [God] to forgive our sins, for verily we were sinners!"
>
> [Jacob] said, "I will seek the forgiveness of my Lord for you, for He is indeed the Oft-Forgiving, the Merciful."
>
> Then when they entered the presence of Joseph, he made a home for his parents with himself and said, "[I bid] you enter Egypt, by God's leave, with safety."
>
> And he raised his parents high on the throne, and they [all] fell down in prostration before him. He said, "O my father! This is the meaning of my vision of old! God has made it true! He was indeed good to me when He freed me from prison and brought you [all] here from the desert after Satan had put enmity between me and my brothers. Truly my Lord is Subtle [in unveiling] whatever He wills! Verily He is the Knowing, the Wise." (from *surat yusuf* / "Joseph" [12]:90–100)

The brothers, now absolved, experience a total transformation of situation, and they are reconciled with their brother and are finally able to accept his privileged status without envy. Satan (the whisperer) is blamed for having inspired their evil deeds. While a case could have been made for a harsher ruling by which justice might have come close to vengeance, love and forgiveness are shown to be infinitely better. In this light, then, we read other Qur'anic passages stressing God's preference for forgiveness and reconciliation:

> Hold to forgiveness; command what is right, and turn away from the ignorant. (from *surat al-a'raf* / "the heights" [7]:199)

Even while the Qur'an allows for the "law of equality" (i.e., the grim and literal justice of exacting an eye for an eye), with the reminder that this primitive form of justice restrains people from perpetrating violence against each other so acts as a positive force in human affairs (*surat al-baqara* / "the cow" [2]:177–179), it emphasizes that God has opened another, better path for dealing with situations of injury and loss, and this is the path of remission, compensation, and reconciliation. Stating undeniable preference for this second way, the Qur'ān explains that God offers it as a concession and token of Divine mercy. Other texts and precedent-setting prophetic acts corroborate this, as we will see below.

It is crucial to understand that the Qur'ān gives a choice to the one who has suffered injury and/or loss: to seek justice or to seek reconciliation and transformation. In other words, the injured party is empowered to choose, with a strong word of encouragement to think seriously about God's preferred option. Forgiveness and reconciliation are thus not mandated or forced upon the injured; rather, both paths are left open. In years of working with people who have suffered loss and trauma, this point has taken on great significance for me. When a person's power has been taken from her or him through violence, she or he must regain a sense of wholeness and personal empowerment before the option of forgiveness has any meaning. In the case of Joseph, he forgave from a place of power and healing, and we see an almost identical dynamic in the life of the prophet Muhammad.

After three major battles and a few smaller skirmishes with his Meccan adversaries, Muhammad had established something close to a military parity between his adopted city of Medina and his hostile hometown of Mecca. At this point, he boldly led a sizeable group of Muslim companions (over a thousand, the report relates) to Mecca, where they intended to make the minor pilgrimage ('umrah) and worship God at the Abrahamic shrine of the Ka'ba. Before they reached the city, they were stopped at a place called Hudaybiyah by representatives of the Meccans, who wanted to prevent Muhammad and his companions from entering the city. Much to the consternation of many of his companions, Muhammad agreed to postpone the pilgrimage for a year as part of a peace treaty he negotiated with a Meccan representative there on the spot. The treaty included a non-aggression pact for ten years, as well as Muhammad's promise to send back any young Meccan who came to him as a convert without the explicit permission of his Meccan father or guardian. On the other side, any Muslim or resident of Medina wanting to seek asylum in Mecca would not be sent back.

For this and other reasons, many of his companions—including 'Umar ibn al-Khaṭṭāb, who would later become the second of the "Rightly-Guided Caliphs"—voiced very strong objections to the Prophet's decision, but he went ahead anyway, commanding the Muslims to abide by every bit of it. What they did not know was that Islam would spread considerably while the treaty was in effect and that, once the treaty was violated and dissolved a few years later, it gave justification for the Muslims to march on Mecca to take the city without bloodshed. More will be said of this below.

This telling episode demonstrated to Muhammad's companions and to all future Muslim leaders that the Prophet, as leader, was not be accountable to their wishes, no matter how strongly felt or voiced. Instead, he was bound by a higher accountability, which included the higher goods of peace, security, and the eventual winning of Mecca without violence. This admittedly difficult element of Muslim leadership has challenged Muslim leaders of every place and time, but I think contemporary Muslim leaders—indeed all religious leaders—are especially challenged to ponder the implications of this principle, so powerfully illustrated by the pact or "Treaty" of al-Hudaybiyah. In what ways are religious leaders challenged to go against the wishes of their communities in order to promote a higher good? Is being sensitive and responsive to our communities the same as being obedient to their wishes and demands? If so, then who is leading whom? In what ways does our accountability to God cause us to clash with the wishes of those we are supposed to lead? These and other questions naturally arise from the Prophet's decisive turn from military action to negotiation and beyond.

As intimated above, a violation of the "Treaty of al-Huday-biya" finally brought Muhammad back to his hometown (Mecca) with an overwhelming force. Mecca surrendered unconditionally, and so its inhabitants, after years of supporting a war to extermi-nate Muhammad, his followers, and his monotheistic movement, were finally cornered, powerless, and completely at his mercy. Of course, the Meccans feared the worst and yet hoped for mercy as they watched him enter the ancient shrine town associated with Abraham, Ishmael, and Hagar. According to the earliest biograph-ical accounts, in the midst of that dramatic first day back in his hometown of Mecca, a day in which he cleansed the Ka'ba of its many idols, Muhammad asked his long-time foes, "What do you think I shall do to you now? They replied that they hoped he—be-ing a "noble brother" and relative—would be gracious to them. Thereupon Muhammad is reported to have consciously connected his situation with that of the prophet Joseph (Yusuf) as he said, "Today I shall say to you what Joseph said to his brothers: 'Today there is no blame on you.' Go, you are all free."[4] In some parallel early accounts, he is reported to have said more simply, "Go your way; you are freed."[5]

In the wake of this act of mercy and forgiveness, the people of Mecca enthusiastically embraced Islam, and the Ka'ba was cleansed and rededicated as "the house" of God, *Allāh*. The mercy and forgiveness celebrated in the Qur'ānic depiction of God and in the stories of the prophets (esp. Joseph) became manifest in their midst, and the immediate result was the reunification of families and the forward march of an expanded and united Muslim *um-mah*. When viewed in the context of the Prophet's life, then, we can see that conflict led to negotiation, which led to forgiveness and the eventual transformation of both the wronged and the wrongdoers.

4. One twentieth-century source that preserves this traditional account is Martin Lings' *Muhammad*.

5. See F. E. Peters, *Muhammad and the Origins of Islam*, 236–37, where he quotes the very early biography by Ibn Ishāq and translated by Alfred Guillaume, *Life of Muhammad*, 550–53.

Qur'ānically, then, it would seem that human affairs, even in the aftermath of great injustices, offenses, and many episodes of mortal combat, can only find resolution and renewal when they emulate the pattern that God has decreed for Godself and celebrated in the lives of the messengers. While conventional justice always remains an option for the injured, it promises no transformation, only perhaps a grim sense of satisfaction that does not advance us toward the supreme goal. Reconciliation—when chosen freely—promises the simultaneous transformation of all parties, the injured and the perpetrator, and so unveils the power and mystery of Divine mercy in the midst of human history.

The Qur'ānic admission of armed conflict cannot be understood outside of this larger context. In the Qur'ān, God is Peace, and God is Justice, and God is Holy. War can thus never be holy, even though it may at times be necessary to combat oppression, which the Qur'an says is the greater evil (2:217).

LINGERING QUESTIONS ARISING FROM MEDINA

In becoming the shaper and leader of a city-state and then an expanding society, did Muhammad establish a religious obligation for all future Muslims to bear? In other words, does following his example necessitate the establishment of an alternative society or state, where the laws are based upon scriptural rulings and religious principles? Some twentieth-century activists, including Ayatollah Khomeini and Sayyid Qutb, emphatically answer in the affirmative. Or was Muhammad forced by the specific conditions of his own circumstances to establish a political union that would enable him to protect and grow the monotheistic faith and way of life? If this latter point is granted, does it mean that—barring those hostile and intimidating circumstances—Muslims need not pursue statehood when their situation is more favorable, allowing them to assemble and practice their faith freely and fully and without coercion? As we mentioned above, many contemporary

Muslims, including prominent Muslim scholars in both the East and the West, emphatically argue this to be so. Indeed, some even go as far as to say that Islam can only truly exist today in a secular or religiously neutral environment, where religion is disconnected from the coercive power of the manmade, imperfect state.[6] One of the Qur'ānic justifications for this is the famous injunction that there can be no coercion in matters of religion (*sūra[t] al-baqara* / "the cow" [2]:256).

Turning away from the question of statehood and to the interrelated questions of violence, injury, forgiveness, and transformation, what kinds of challenges do the Qur'ān and the prophetic record pose for Muslims today? Has justice come to mean vengeance for some who cry out for the rule of Islamic Law in the contemporary world? What are the theaters, both personal and political, that desperately cry out for the kind of transformation found in the story of Joseph and in the prophet Muhammad's own legacy? How might this be achieved? Are Muslim communities ready to seek this transformation, or—disregarding God's clear preference for compensation and reconciliation—will some stick to their own preferences and conceptions of justice, which may promise no transformation? These are some of the questions that fuel contemporary Muslim discussions and debates across the globe, and the one thing we can say with fair certitude is that every argument and line of reasoning traces back to Medina, to the Prophet's legacy and to its relevance for the contemporary world. Medina, then, is not so much a historical reality as it is a living archetype for Muslims of every place and time.

6. For example, see Abdullahi Ahmed An-Na'im's *Islam and the Secular State.*

Section IV

Experience

As for the boat, it belonged to poor men who worked on the sea. I wanted to make it defective [because] there was behind them a king who was seizing all boats by force.

As for the young man, his parents were believers, and we dreaded that he would overburden them by oppression [and cruelty] and ingratitude. So we desired that their Lord would give them in exchange one better in purity and closer [to them] in sympathy.

As for the wall, it belonged to two orphaned youths in the city; [buried] beneath it was a treasure that belonged to them: their father had been a righteous man, and so your Lord wished that the two [boys], [when] they came of age, find it and excavate their treasure as a mercy from your Lord. Thus, I did not do it of my own [accord]. That, then, is the true interpretation of that concerning which you were unable to hold patience.

~ The Qur'ān, from the *sūra* of the Cave / *al-kahf* (18):79–82

9

Pursuing Ultimate Horizons

The Mysteries of Being and Becoming "Muslim"[1]

"And We shall show them Our signs in the horizons and in themselves."

~ The Qur'ān: *hā mīm* (41):53

According to a report given by Abū Hurayra (may God be pleased with him) and recorded in the ḥadīth collection of al-Bukhārī, the Prophet (may God's prayers and blessings be upon him) said,

God said: "My servant draws near to Me by nothing more beloved to Me than that which I have enjoined upon him [i.e., the religious duties], and My servant continues to draw nigh unto Me with extra, voluntary devotions so that I [come to] love him. When I love him, I am his hearing by which he hears, his seeing by which he sees, his hand with which

---

1. While original in many ways, this section draws heavily on the "Islamic View of Humanity," a short chapter I wrote some years ago for the volume, *On Human Nature*. Parts have also been inspired by a more recent presentation I made at the *Journey to Ihsan Second International Conference on Islamic Spirituality* sponsored by Abdul Aleem Siddique Mosque, Singapore, Sept. 2006.

he strikes and his foot with which he walks. Were he to ask [something] of Me, I would surely give it to him, and were he to ask Me for refuge, I would surely grant it." (*Ṣaḥīḥ al-Bukhārī*, bk. 76 —*kitāb al-riqāq* / "*the book of making the heart tender*" (no. 509).

∾

WHILE ATTENDING *an interfaith conference in Amritsar, India, a few years ago, I sought out a mosque on Friday afternoon so that I could observe my Friday prayers and meet some of the Muslims in this predominantly Sikh city of the Punjab. The sermon was—surprisingly—in Arabic, which was good for me but perhaps not very helpful to the thousands of everyday people who were there in attendance that day. For them, a Punjabi sermon would have been far more useful, I thought. In any case, after prayers, I spent some time walking through the city with a young Kashmiri man I met at the mosque, and we began to talk about life in India, life in Canada, life in the United States. Of course the visa question came up, as it always does, but, beyond that, the only religious question he asked me was whether it was permissible to watch World Federation Wrestling on TV. I told him that, while such entertainment was not explicitly prohibited, it was certainly not the best way to spend his time. After days of inspiring interfaith conversation with Muslim, Jewish, Christian, Hindu, Buddhist, and Sikh religious leaders and scholars, the question hit me fairly hard. "How we are failing our youth!" I thought. "We have to give them more than this!"*

In the course of another trip just a year before in neighboring Pakistan, the same message came to me in a different form. I was having a wonderful time: making friends with colleagues and students at the International Islamic University in Islamabad (IIUI), receiving wonderful treatment everywhere I went, being stopped and embraced by soldiers and police officers who were thrilled to discover an American brother dressed in their traditional shalwar-qamis garment and in pursuit of religious learning and collaboration, etc.

One day, as I walked in the afternoon heat and past a hotel (a good two stars fancier than the one where I was staying), I encountered a white-robed man from one of the Gulf countries. As is my custom, I smiled at him and greeted him in Arabic, "as-salaamu 'alaykum!" He looked at me scornfully and tersely replied, "wa 'alaykum"—a clear indication that he doubted my sincerity or held me in some kind of contempt or suspicion.

Rather than being happy to meet me, he immediately began criticizing my beard, which he said was in clear contradiction of the Prophet's custom and the requirements of the faith. I thanked him for his concern and went on to explain that Muslim scholars and sages have always upheld a distinction between what is required (farḍ) and what is optional, even recommended (usually involving the sunnah, or prophetic custom). He would hear none of it. "Everything is farḍ," he said. "To depart from any custom of the Prophet—God's peace and blessings be upon him—is tantamount to forsaking the religion." I tried to convince him that there was much more to this religion than the shape of one's beard, that this should not even be a matter of discussion while innocents are being killed in the name of the religion, while so many millions of people go without adequate food and shelter, etc. I explained that, on Judgment Day, if this is the greatest of the sins held against me, I will be a happy man. He had no patience for anything I said.

Finally, when it was clear that the two of us were not going to come to a place of agreement on anything, I thanked him again and wished him peace. Even more scornful than he was at the outset of our exchange, he barked out the formal reply and stormed off. As he walked away, a hotel doorman, who had been listening to the entire conversation, came up and said to me in an awed voice, "That is a real Muslim." Feeling as if he had just slugged me in the stomach, and yet outraged by this reduction of the religion to the cut of one's beard or the shape of one's outfit, I took a deep breath and began explaining to this doorman that Islam—real Islam—has to go much deeper than the façade of our external appearance . . . After all, what good *is the beard or the robe if we are not surrendering our hearts to God? What good is the prayer if we are not feeding the poor, sheltering the homeless, caring for the sick, and working for a better world, as the Qur'an commands? Instead, we say our prayers and strut around like peacocks, picking at people's beards and headscarves while people starve on the street or get blown up by misguided youth . . . He looked at me as if I was from Mars. I guess he had never heard anyone talk about religion in this way, and he wasn't quite sure what to make of me, let alone of my strange religious perspective.*

∼

In this little book, we have reflected upon fundamental aspects of Islamic history, Islamic theology, and Islamic practice, but so far we have not really taken up the question of religious experience, a more personal perspective that integrates all these aspects and yet is much more than the sum of their parts. What might it *feel* like to be an observant Muslim, to submit oneself daily to this rigor of discipline and remembrance? What does contemporary life look like when viewed through the lens of the ancient Arabic text of the Qur'ān and the traditions of the Prophet, a man who lived in a very different time and culture? What does it mean for a pious Muslim to be living her life as a "return" journey to God, with whom lies the mystery of every person's origin and innate disposition (*fiṭra*), and also the mystery of his/her ultimate destiny or realization? While the specific answers to these questions always differ somewhat from individual to individual, I will try, in this final chapter, to describe the interior landscape or "theater" where these questions and mysteries play out.

If this "theater" were to have a name that would be meaningful for all Muslims everywhere, that name would be *al-iḥsān*—sometimes translated as "righteousness." For this is the "station" of transformative awareness that one is in the constant presence of the Divine. *Al-iḥsān* thus embraces every aspect of human existence and reconnects it to God. In this way, scholars (such as William Chittick) have said that *al-ihsān* stands for the perfection of both the religion and the self. In doing so, it heightens, expands, intensifies, and illuminates one's entire understanding of the faith and the practice, and it also does this for the believer's evolving understanding of his or her own true nature.

The lived Islamic life, then, when informed and illumined by this transformative awareness, flows from a fundamental mystery. The core of that mystery is the human heart, understood to be a kind of universe in itself, a universe in which the believer is said to encounter the Divine. "We are closer to him [i.e., the human person] than his own jugular vein," says the Qur'ān (50:16). Connected with this are several evocative statements attributed to the prophet Muhammad, who is reported to have anchored the mystery of Divine proximity in the human heart: the hearts of all people are "between two of the Merciful's fingers," one such tradition says (see *Ṣaḥīḥ* Muslim [no. 2654]).[2] Another reported prophetic saying, less authenticated but still very popular in both Sunni and Shī'ī spiritual traditions, relates God saying, "Nothing in My earth or My heaven can contain Me; however, the heart of My believing servant contains Me."[3] The general thrust of these and other Islamic texts is that our human nature, at its very core, is believed to be somehow in direct touch with the Divine, and for this reason the human heart or spirit is left undefined in Islam, indeed just as God is left undefined, known only by attributes that

---

2. Similar traditions can be found in the collections of Ibn Mājah, Aḥmad ibn Ḥanbal, and al-Tirmidhī.

3. This tradition is widely quoted in the spiritual literature of both medieval and contemporary Islam. See, for example, the medieval Persian spiritual treatise, "Rising Places of Faith," translated by William Chittick in *Faith and Practice of Islam*, 24. While it is difficult to pin down a canonical primary source for this tradition, it is cited by Abū Ḥāmid al-Ghazālī and Ibn al-'Arabī among many others.

reflect aspects of the Divine nature but never capture the totality of God's essence.[4]

Interestingly, this ambiguity concerning the true nature of the spiritual "heart" or spirit was put to the test during the Prophet's own lifetime. Of the many groups and individuals who resisted and resented Muhammad's claim to prophecy in the seventh century, some sought to confound him with religious and spiritual questions of considerable nuance and subtlety. One of the most famous of these questions concerned the spirit or soul. According to the account of the earliest biographer of the Prophet, when Muhammad was pressed to explain the spirit's true nature, he waited, seeking God's help. Divine help eventually came, but in a way that raised more questions than it answered. The Qur'ānic verse in question simply said, "They ask you concerning the spirit: say, 'the spirit is of my Lord's command. Of knowledge, what you have been given is little'" (al-Isrā' [17]: 85).[5] The Prophet offered them nothing more than this, and his companions and subsequent generations of followers all agreed that the Prophet's restraint in this matter was binding upon them all. In this way, the Islamic tradition came to cover the mystery of the spirit or soul with a heavy silence. Ever after, the matter was referred to as the "secret of the spirit" and was deemed to be among the restricted topics concerning which open discussion and speculation were forbidden.

This is not to say that the topic was wholly forgotten by the tradition. Indeed, some of the most renowned and influential masters of classical/medieval Islam deemed an understanding of the spirit's secret to be among the most important religious insights, albeit one that could never be shared with others. One such master who deserves a place in our discussion is Abū Ḥāmid

4. This explicit admission of the ultimate transcendence and unknowability of the Divine is recalled many times every day for Muslims, who repeat the cry "God is greater" ("Allāhu Akbar") multiple times in their daily devotions (al-ṣalāh). See above, esp. chapter 3.

5. For more information concerning the context and interpretation of this verse, see my al-Ghazālī's Unspeakable Doctrine of the Soul, 1–2.

al-Ghazālī (d. 1111 CE), a widely-known and respected scholar
of jurisprudence and dogmatic theology who, in the very midst
of a flourishing career in Baghdad, abandoned his professorship
and secluded himself in order to devote himself to a path of inner
purification and experiential/mystical knowledge. As he matured
and grew in the light of this spiritual knowledge, he wrote copi-
ously and composed the work that would later be regarded as his
magnum opus—Reviving Religious Knowledge (Iḥyā' 'ulūm al-dīn),
essentially a forty-book manual for spiritual formation in Islam.[6]

Here, in the book entitled *The Commentary on the Wonders
of the Heart*, he writes: "the true knowledge of the [true nature of
the] heart and of the reality of its distinguishing characteristics is
the very basis of religion and the foundation for the spiritual path
of those making their way [to God]."[7] Later, in the final volume
entitled *The Remembrance of Death and the Afterlife*, he writes:

> It is impossible to remove the covering from the true nature of
> the reality of death, since death cannot be known by one who
> does not understand life, and the true knowledge of life is [at-
> tained] through the knowledge of the true nature of the spirit
> in its essence and through grasping the quiddity of its essence.
> [However,] it was not permitted for [even] the Emissary of
> God (may God bless him and grant him salvation) to speak
> of this, nor to say more than "the spirit is of my Lord's com-
> mand." Thus it is not for any of the doctors of religion to reveal
> the secret of the spirit, even if one were to come to know it.
> Indeed, all that is permitted is the mentioning of the state of
> the spirit after death.[8]

THE SOUL AS A RECEPTACLE OF KNOWLEDGE, SPECIFICALLY THE KNOWLEDGE OF GOD, ONE'S

6. Throughout the remainder of this chapter, I base all translations on the
Arabic text annotated by al-Imām al-Ḥāfiẓ al-'Irāqī.

7. Ghazālī, *Iḥyā'*, 3:112.

8. Ibid., 6:132.

ORIGIN, AND ONE'S ULTIMATE RETURN

But what are we, really? What is our fundamental nature as creatures of the Divine? If the heart can only be defined tentatively in terms of attributes and states, then what are its attributes and states? Certainly one of the most exalted and defining attributes of our human nature is knowledge—knowledge of ourselves, the world around us, and, most importantly, knowledge of God.

According to the Qur'ān, when God was just about to create Adam, the angels objected, asking, "What! Are you going to place in the earth one who will do mischief and shed blood while we celebrate your praises and proclaim your holiness?" God responded with a simple, enigmatic line, "I know what you know not" (2:30). Then God created Adam, established him as God's own vicegerent on the earth, and taught him "the names, all of them" (2:31).[9] After doing this, God turned to the angels and asked them to recite for Him the names. They, of course, had no such knowledge, and so they said, "We have no knowledge save that which you have taught us" (2:32). God then commanded Adam to tell them the names, and Adam did. Thereupon the angels were commanded to bow down before him (2:34). This Qur'ānic story illustrates for Muslims God's favoring of humanity with the attribute of knowledge—an attribute that elevates the human being above even the rank of the angels. Knowledge then represents not only one of the attributes of God, but a Divine quality in which humans can have a share due to the mercy and inscrutable wisdom of the Divine. The pursuit of this knowledge is thus the quintessential human aspiration, and its attainment marks human fulfillment and perfection.

---

9. Exactly what these "names" pertain to remains something of a mystery. In some Islamic texts, they are taken to be the Divine names or attributes, while, in others, they are seen as having to do with the essential natures of everything to be found within the created realm, of which Adam is seen as the primordial steward or vicegerent (*khalīfa*). See, for example, Ibn al-'Arabī, *Bezels of Wisdom*, esp. 50–59.

Beyond this innate potential for knowing the mysteries of the creation, Muslims believe that all human beings already possess some knowledge of God. In fact, the knowledge of God is believed to have been woven into the very fabric of human nature. Giving evidence for this, the Qur'ān tells of a most inexplicable episode long ago—in fact prior to the creation itself. Prior to our very existence, save in the Divine mind, God is said to have summoned us all out of nonexistence to stand before Him for a moment that would mark us for all eternity. In this meeting, God asked all the souls who would ever come into existence a simple and direct question: "Am I not your Lord?" In unison, all the souls replied, "Aye, we do testify" (7:172). Thus, according to what we may call the spiritual psychology of Islam, when a human being gazes deeply enough into his or her own heart, he or she will find the memory of that meeting.

Aside from the attributes discussed above, the Islamic tradition acknowledges that the heart is often in an unsteady state. The Qur'ān stresses that God created the human person in the best possible form or constitution (*fī aḥsani taqwīm*), a form said to be modeled after God's own image;[10] however, it is also stressed that even the most exalted condition can plummet to "the lowest of the low" if one rejects God's blessings and signs and does evil (95). This illustrates for us one of the most fundamental insights Islam brings to our discussion of human nature: the heart—or essence of the human being—is a magnificent yet volatile thing. In fact, the root meaning of "heart" (*al-qalb*) in Arabic is to "turn over," "roll

10. The idea that the human person is created in God's image, while reminiscent of the biblical teaching (Gen 1:27), comes into Islam from a universally accepted *ḥadīth* tradition, in which the Prophet is reported to have said, "God created Adam according to His image (*'alā ṣūratihi*)." See al-Bukhari, bk. 74, no. 246. Because the possessive pronoun in Arabic is, of course, not capitalized (there are no capital letters in Arabic) and comes in the form of a generic, third person masculine possessive suffix, there is room for divergent readings. Our reading (above) is the most widely accepted, although mainstream commentators are careful to remind us that there is nothing like unto God.

over," or "flip." Indeed, one of the modern words for "revolution" in Arabic (*inqilāb*) comes from the same root, as do a great many other words implying change, circularity, and fluctuation. In one well authenticated prophetic tradition, cited above, we find the Prophet calling upon God as the "Turner of Hearts" (*Muqallib al-qulūb*) and saying, "the hearts of the believers are between the two fingers of the Merciful." This is found in numerous reports and in a few variations.[11] In other words, the heart can turn in an instant if God were to will it:

> O you who believe! Answer God and His Messenger when He calls you to that which will give you life, and know that God intervenes between a man and his heart and that to Him you shall [all] be gathered. (8:24)

~

THE JOURNEY TO GOD AS BOTH A HOMECOMING AND A BECOMING

When we call to mind the mysterious Qur'ānic reference to a "moment" in the Divine presence prior to the creation itself (7:172), it becomes more understandable why Muslims often refer to the journey to God as a "return." This is reinforced by many Qur'ānic passages that similarly cast the human journey as a return. The adventure of human life can also be described as a process of becoming, a journey from a less authentic and partial nature into a more authentic, fuller nature. This is a process that entails a gradual shedding of one's false and flawed nature and a simultaneous adding of a more "Divine" nature. Although, for nearly all schools of Islamic thought, the separation between Creator and creature is essential and thus permanent,[12] still the perceived

---

11. See, for example, *Ṣaḥīḥ* Muslim, bk. 33, no. 6418.

12. See al-Ghazālī, *Ninety-Nine Beautiful Names of God*, 149–56.

distance between God and human can be lessened, and intimate companionship and conversation are believed to be possible.[13] In addition to the power of Divine grace, this is achieved through the gradual "clothing" of oneself with the Divine names or attributes (to the extent that it is humanly possible), such as we saw with the attribute of knowledge above.

> He is God, besides whom there is no god. He knows the un-seen and the visible, and he is ever Merciful, ever Gracious. He is God, besides whom there is no god. The Sovereign, the Holy, Peace, the ever-Faithful, the Protector, the Mighty, the All-Compelling, the Awe-Inspiring; Exalted is God above everything they associate with God. He is Allāh, the Creator, the Maker, the Fashioner. To Him belong the Most Beautiful Names; everything in the heavens and on the earth proclaims His glory, and He is the Mighty, the Wise. (59:22–24)

The Qur'ān says, "the most beautiful names belong to God; so call on Him by them" (7:180). The sacred text also says that the best raiment for the human being is the raiment of God-consciousness or *taqwā* (7:26). Taking this a step further, the Prophet is reported to have coached his companions to put on or manifest the qualities of God Most High. On another occasion, the Prophet is reported to have said that whosoever extols and acts upon God's attributes will surely enter Heaven.[14] While traditional Muslim scholars and luminaries, such as al-Ghazālī, have cautioned Muslims to understand that they will only ever be able to acquire for themselves something *resembling* God's attributes (not the Divine attributes as they truly are in relation to the Divine), the psycho-spiritual process of coming into one's full nature is the same. It requires the shedding of all ungodly attributes (ultimately even the shedding of personal will), and the slow and steady taking on of God's qualities, including mercy (the Merciful), compassion (the Compassionate),

13. See David Burrell's wonderful chapter on "Friendship with God in al-Ghazali and Aquinas" in *Friendship and Ways to Truth*.

14. See *Ṣaḥīḥ* Bukhari, bk. 75, no. 419; a related version of this appears in bk. 50, no. 894.

forgiveness (the Forgiving), patience and forbearance (the Patient, the Forbearing), gratitude (the Giver of Thanks), wisdom (the Wise), knowledge (the Knowing), peace (Peace), generosity (the Giver of Bounty), justice (Justice), loving-kindness (the Loving), trustworthiness (The Trustee), steadiness of mind and heart (the Eternal, Absolute), etc. In this way, the heart is said to become a polished mirror in which the Divine qualities are reflected rather than being an independent possessor of the Divine qualities.

For example, in reference to the servant's "donning" of the name "Allāh"—God, the name that encompasses all of the other qualities of Lordship and Divinity—al-Ghazālī says that this entails becoming completely consumed with one's remembrance of God, seeing no power or agency in the universe save God's, placing all of one's hopes and ambitions in God, etc. "How could it be otherwise?" he asks, "for it had already been understood from this name that He [God] is the truly actual Existent, and that everything other than He is ephemeral, perishing, and worthless except in relation to Him. [The servant] sees himself first of all as the first of the perishing and the worthless, as did the Messenger of God— may God's grace and peace be upon him."[15]

For the purpose of this gradual transformation and exaltation of our human nature, the remembrance of God and His attributes is perhaps the most characteristically Islamic practice, for it includes and permeates all of the obligatory devotions that shape a Muslim's life. As the Qur'ān commands,

> O you who believe! Keep God ever in mind, and glorify Him morning and evening. He is the one Who blesses you, in concert with His angels, that He may bring you out of the [various] darknesses and into the light: and He has ever been merciful to the believers. Their greeting on the day they meet Him will be "Peace!" And He has prepared for them a gracious reward. O Prophet! We have sent you as a witness, as a bearer of glad tidings, as a warner, and as one who calls [humanity]

---

15. Al-Ghazālī, *Ninety-Nine Beautiful Names of God*, 52; See also R. J. McCarthy's partial translation of the treatise in *Deliverance from Error*, 297.

to God, by God's leave; and [we have sent you] as a shining
lamp. So give glad tidings to the believers that they have a
great blessing [in store] from God. (33:41–47)

Although the various psycho-spiritual states and stations of
one making their way to God may be beyond numbering, the spiritual tradition generally describes the soul's ascent in three broad
stages, all of which are firmly anchored in Qur'ānic descriptions of
soul types: the stage of the soul inclined toward mischief/evil (see
12:53), the penitent soul (75:2), and the soul that has come to rest,
at peace with God (89:27–30). This latter stage is what we may
call the highest expression of human nature, the stage at which the
wayfarer comes home to hear the blessed words, "O soul at rest!
Return to your Lord in a manner both pleasing and well pleased.
Then enter among My servants; enter My paradise."

∿

CONCLUSION

So what is the mystery of human existence and the religious life
when viewed in the light of the station of *al-iḥsān*? The Qur'ān, the
Prophet, and even the ensuing scholarly and mystical traditions
seem to leave the question open, suggesting an innate potential that
would rise even above the ranks of the angels. This is accompanied
by a stern warning, which promises a rank below even the basest of
creatures, except for those who believe and work righteous deeds,
"for to them belongs a reward unlimited" (94:4–6). Are there then
separate and competing human natures, or is volatility itself a kind
of singular nature that slides along a great scale or spectrum of
existence? The answer is not plain.

One thing is clear, however. These Islamic traditions tell us
that, as human beings, our nature involves a directional aspect.
And, for the Muslim, this brings a person back to the question
of lifelong study and daily practice, for knowing these mysteries

theoretically is not enough. What really counts is being on the path to one's higher nature, taking the slow and steady steps prescribed by God and exemplified by the Prophet, who is extolled in the Qur'ān as a "beautiful role model" (*uswa hasana*): "You have indeed in God's messenger a beautiful role model for any one whose hope is in God and the Last Day and who engages much in the Praise of God" (33:21).

It is in the mystery of surrendering oneself wholly to God that a person can rightly be called a *Muslim*—in the company of all of the prophets and true servants who have surrendered themselves to God throughout history. The perfection of this active surrender is being a *Muḥsin*—one who lives and acts in a continual state of *al-iḥsān*, a state in which every waking moment is illuminated by the conscious awareness of God's presence. When beheld in this light, then, the religion of Islam can be understood as a way or path to this higher existence, in which the human being manifests the true nature God created within us, a nature that is intimately connected with the mystery of God's own nature. The religious journey is thus not understood to be a homecoming to God only, but also a homecoming to one's self in the highest sense, albeit a "self" whose essence or true nature defies clear description or even imagining. Whatever it may be, this nature can only ever be found in or with the Divine, who is understood to be both the ultimate origin and the final destination of everyone.

Epilogue

A Few Thoughts on Moses, the Mystic Fish, and Spiritual Education

WHILE MANY points of belief, history, and practice may be clear or becoming clear at this point of our reading and contemplation, there remains a good chance that the reader is still puzzled by the Qur'ānic parable of Moses that has been narrated in stages throughout this little book. Here, at the end, I would like to offer a few thoughts on the meaning and significance of this story for us and for all who study religion and, in doing so, seek a definitive understanding of what it is and how it works.

One of the most striking elements of this parable is that Moses—the great, law-bringing prophet who spoke directly with God and led the descendents of Jacob (Israel) out of captivity and to the borders of their biblical inheritance—is constantly tempted to judge events and people by his own limited observation and partial understanding of the situation at hand. As one of the best and brightest imaginable representatives of humankind, he is required by the mysterious spirit-guide to be patient and refrain from asking any questions, which of course he cannot do. Finally, following his third breach of contract, he is taught a lesson before he is sent away: the realities of life are quite often profoundly different from what they seem; outer appearances are often misleading and deceiving. Behind the veneer of this world and its events there exists an alternate and more comprehensive unfolding, which is providential, guided by a Divine "logic" that is, to our limited field of vision, random and incomprehensible.

Moses is thus taught to walk humbly and to refrain from his tendency to judge events according to a finite number of superficial factors. While the story does not follow Moses after he and his spirit-guide part ways, we may well imagine that he emerged from this experience somewhat altered in his perspective, deeply pensive, pondering the mystery of life, and marked by the spiritual virtue of epistemological humility—the disposition of one who knows that he does not fully know. Mysteriously, then, we find that the end of his journey into knowledge became identical to the beginning, for, at both, the great law-bringing Prophet was a spiritual seeker who manifested the Qur'ānic supplication, "O my Lord! Increase me in knowledge!" (20:114).

My concluding wish or hope, therefore, is that this little book will return us to the beginning and so serve as a call to seek more knowledge and to be wary of the temptation to judge things prematurely, to convict on circumstantial evidence, to "essentialize" or reduce Islam, or any other way of faith, to a finite collection of selected, observable "facts." Religion is always more than the sum of its parts, and Islam is no exception.

Bibliography

Ahmed, Leila. *Women and Gender in Islam*. Oxford: Oxford University Press, 1992.

An-Na'im, Abdullahi Ahmed. *Islam and the Secular State: Negotiating the Future of Shari'ah*. Cambridge, MA: Harvard University Press, 2008.

Arberry, A. J. *The Seven Odes: the First Chapter in Arabic Literature*. London: George Allen & Unwin, 1957.

Burrell, David. *Friendship and Ways to Truth*. Notre Dame, Indiana: University of Notre Dame Press, 2000.

Chittick, William. *The Faith and Practice of Islam: Three Thirteenth Century Sufi Texts*. Albany, NY: State University of New York Press, 1992.

Denny, Frederick. "Pre-Islamic Arabia: Beliefs, Values, Way of Life." In *An Introduction to Islam*, 29–43. 3rd ed. Upper Saddle River, NJ: Pearson Education, 2006.

Donohue, John J., and John Esposito, eds. *Islam in Transition: Muslim Perspectives*. 2nd ed. New York: Oxford University Press, 2007.

Esack, Farid. *The Qur'an: A User's Guide*. Oxford: Oneworld Publications, 2005.

Fakhry, Majid. *A History of Islamic Philosophy*. 3rd ed. New York: Columbia University Press, 2004.

Feiler, Bruce. *Abraham: A Journey to the Heart of Three Faiths*. New York: HarperCollins, 2002.

Firestone, Reuven. "Abraham's Association with the Meccan Sanctuary and the Pilgrimage in the Pre-Islamic and Early Islamic Periods." *Le Museon Revue d'Etudes Orientales* 104 (1991), 365–93.

———. *Journeys in Holy Lands: The Evolution of the Abraham-Ishmael Legends in Islamic Exegesis*. Albany, NY: SUNY Press, 1990.

———. "Patriarchy, Primogeniture and Polemic in the Exegetical Traditions of Judaism and Islam." In *Jewish Biblical Interpretation and Cultural Exchange: Comparative Exegesis in Context*, edited by David Stern and Natalie Dohrmann, 108–23. Philadelphia: University of Pennsylvania Press, 2008.

Bibliography

Ghazālī, Abū Ḥāmid al-. *The Alchemy of Happiness*. Translated by Claud Field. London: M. E. Sharpe, 1991.

———. *The Ninety-Nine Beautiful Names of God*. Translated and with notes by David B. Burrell and Nazih Daher. Louisville, KY: Islamic Texts Society, 1992[1995]).

———. *Reviving Religious Knowledge* (*Ihyā' 'ulūm al-dīn*). Edited by al-Imām al-Ḥāfiẓ al-'Irāqī. Beirut: Dār al-khayr, 1993.

Gianotti, Timothy J. *Al-Ghazālī's Unspeakable Doctrine of the Soul: Unveiling the Esoteric Psychology and Eschatology of the Ihyā'*. Leiden: E. J. Brill, 2001.

———. "The Islamic View of Humanity." In *On Human Nature: the Jerusalem Center Symposium*, edited by Truman Madsen, David Noel Friedman, and Pam Fox Kuhlken, 85–93. Ann Arbor, MI: Pryor Pettengill, 2004.

Giddens, Anthony. *The Consequences of Modernity*. Stanford: Stanford University Press, 1990.

Guillaume, Alfred. *The Life of Muhammad: A Translation of [Ibn] Ishāq's "Sirat Rasul Allah,"* with introduction and notes. Oxford: Oxford University Press, 1955.

Haley, Alex. *The Autobiography of Malcolm X*. New York: Ballantine Books, 1964, 1965.

Ibn 'Arabi, al-. *The Bezels of Wisdom*. Translated and introduction by R. W. J. Austin. New York: Paulist Press, 1980.

Irwin, Robert, ed. "Pagan Poets." In *Night and Horses and the Desert: The Penguin Anthology of Classical Arabic Literature*, 1–29. London; New York; Toronto: Penguin Books, 2000.

Levenson, Jon D. "Abraham Among Jews, Christians, and Muslims: Monotheism, Exegesis, and Religious Diversity." *ARC* 26 (1998) 5–29.

———. "The Conversion of Abraham to Judaism, Christianity, and Islam." In *The Idea of Biblical Interpretation: Essays in Honor of James L. Kugel*, edited by Hindy Najman and Judith H. Newman, 3–40. Leiden: E. J. Brill, 2004.

Lings, Martin. *Muhammad: His Life Based Upon the Earliest Sources*. Rochester, VT: Inner Traditions, 2006; originally published London: George Allen & Unwin, 1983.

Mattson, Ingrid. *The Story of the Qur'an: Its History and Place in Muslim Life*. Malden, MA: Wiley-Blackwell, 2008

McCarthy, R. J., trans. *Deliverance from Error*. Louisville, KY: Fons Vitae, 1999.

Nicholson, R. A. *A Literary History of the Arabs*. Cambridge: Cambridge University Press, 1969.

Peters, F. E. *Muhammad and the Origins of Islam*. Albany, NY: SUNY Press, 1994.

———. *A Reader on Classical Islam.* Princeton, NJ: Princeton University Press, 1994.

Rahman, Fazlur. *Major Themes of the Qur'ān.* Minneapolis: Bibliotecha Islamica, 1994.

Rubin, Uri. "The Khadija-Waraqa Story." In *The Eye of the Beholder: The Life of Muhammad As Viewed by the Early Muslims*, 103–12. Princeton, NJ: Darwin Press, 1995.

Said, Edward W. *Orientalism.* New York: Vintage, 1979.

Shaheen, Jack. *Reel Bad Arabs: How Hollywood Villifies a People.* New York: Olive Branch Press, 2001.

Watt, W. Montgomery. *Muhammad: Prophet and Statesman.* Oxford: Oxford University Press, 1961.

———. *Muhammad at Mecca.* Oxford: Oxford University Press, 1953. Reprint, Karachi, Pakistan: Oxford University Press, 1980.

———. *Muhammad at Medina.* Oxford: Oxford University Press, 1956. Reprint, Karachi, Pakistan: Oxford University Press, 1981.

∼ Online Resources ∼

For online syllabi, lectures, topically arranged bibliographies, and other resources for exploring Islam and other religions, as well as for news about Dr. Gianotti's public lectures, workshops, courses, reading and discussion groups, interfaith events, and public statements concerning contemporary issues, see:

www.islamicilluminations.com

and

www.islamicilluminations.blogspot.com